# About the Author

was a corporate lawyer who became a negotiator and then a
00 commercial director until one day when he decided to quit
what he loved instead. He faced his fears and left his well-paid
to find out that what scared him kept chasing him about. He
orks with a range of people from creative leaders to primary
children on their quite different but somehow related chal-
For the past couple of years, he has been running Fear Hack
kshops alongside his main work as an enabler of natural growth.
y is also the author of *The Power of Soft – a guide to getting what
vant without being a \*\*\*\**.

allo.com

# FEAR HACK

# FEAR HACK

## HILARY GALLO

Unbound Digital

This edition first published in 2019

Unbound

6th Floor Mutual House, 70 Conduit Street, London W1S 2GF

www.unbound.com

ISBN (eBook): 978-1-78965-011-2
ISBN (Paperback): 978-1-78965-010-5

Cover design by Accept & Proceed

Printed and bound in Great Britain by Clays Ltd, Elcograf S.p.A.

*for fear itself*

*A special thank you to*
*David Johnston and the team at Accept & Proceed*
*who backed this book as a supporting organisation and*
*designed the book cover.*

Dear Reader,

The book you are holding came about in a rather different way to most others. It was funded directly by readers through a new website: Unbound.

Unbound is the creation of three writers. We started the company because we believed there had to be a better deal for both writers and readers. On the Unbound website, authors share the ideas for the books they want to write directly with readers. If enough of you support the book by pledging for it in advance, we produce a beautifully bound special subscribers' edition and distribute a regular edition and e-book wherever books are sold, in shops and online.

This new way of publishing is actually a very old idea (Samuel Johnson funded his dictionary this way). We're just using the internet to build each writer a network of patrons. Here, at the back of this book, you'll find the names of all the people who made it happen.

Publishing in this way means readers are no longer just passive consumers of the books they buy, and authors are free to write the books they really want. They get a much fairer return too – half the profits their books generate, rather than a tiny percentage of the cover price.

If you're not yet a subscriber, we hope that you'll want to join our publishing revolution and have your name listed in one of our books in the future. To get you started, here is a £5 discount on your first pledge. Just visit unbound.com, make your pledge and type FEAR18 in the promo code box when you check out.

Thank you for your support,

Dan, Justin and John
Founders, Unbound

# Super Patrons

Nadya Powell
Wyn Roberts
Fiona Roper
Ian Roper
Jonathan Royle Hypnotist
Lizzy Rudd
Robert Shooter
Jonathan Smith
Eleanor Sturdy
David Thomlinson
Justin Verderber
Jim Walsh
Simon White

'Why are you wearing that stupid bunny suit?'
'Why are you wearing that stupid man suit?'
– *Donnie Darko* (2001)

Most of this book is based on stuff that has happened. Generally, I tell the story of what I remember, from my perspective. I have changed some names and allowed a few animals in. Please don't take the animals, in particular, too seriously. No species, including us, has yet worked out a perfect example of how to live. Sometimes it just helps to use paint to make a picture. It doesn't mean that the paint is there to be licked.

# Contents

# Welcome

The first thing I do when I talk about fear is explain why I'm here in the first place and why fear interests me. Over time, this has become a series of admissions, as the truth has slowly crept its way in. The biggest of these truths is that I don't feel that I ever really chose fear at all. It was more that it kept coming up. It chose me. I'd slowly noticed that a ghostly character lurked in the wings of the stage. It seemed that no one, including me, ever wanted to admit that it was there. This indistinct and frankly rather annoying presence somehow managed to influence all the action, without ever having been given a part in the play.

My first book was about negotiation and I noticed that, whenever I talked about it after it came out, the topic that kept coming up was fear. On the negotiation stage, fear made people positional. It made them defensive of the ground they had taken for themselves, and once they were there, it held them there. Again and again, I noticed how it was fear of one sort or another that tended to lock us all up. This wasn't a fear of anything that would cause us actual harm. It was more of a desire to avoid uncertainty or to fit in. This was social rather than physical. People didn't do the thing they truly wanted to do because they feared doing so would expose them to a risk. Often these risks were small or irrational, yet they consistently felt bigger than they had any rational right to be. We're not going to be killed or threatened with death by asking for the salary we so badly need or speaking out in the meeting we've been passionate enough to attend, but it can feel as if we are.

Faced with the unwelcome visitor of fear, our natural reaction is to pick up our weapons to fight it. In this frame of mind, I'd find myself issuing a stream of daily exhortations to myself and others in my work to be open, to embrace change or to take a stand. There are plenty of people ready to tell us what to do, and I was standing firmly in this stream. As a writer and a speaker, I was full of advice about what one should do. The problem with this is that most of the time we already know what we need to do to be better. I realised that it wasn't a lack of knowing the clear thing to do that was the problem. The problem was not understanding the more shadowy thing that stops us.

One day, after a conversation with a client who'd remained resolutely stuck despite my help, I shifted my focus away from the goal question and got more interested in the big piece of elastic that pulls us back. The important thing was to understand the rather too comfortable and silent force that not only stops us but also contains us. I wanted to know more about the invisible cradling that fear creeps in and puts around us. Understanding that force is a big part of this book, because once we see what stops us, everything else happens so much more easily.

One day, instead of resisting it, I decided to step towards the ghost. As soon as I took the first step, I saw its shapeless presence react. Fear wasn't expecting me to put down my little child's sword and it wasn't expecting to be approached with kindness. As I moved tentatively towards it, I started to learn about it and saw that I'd come to none of the immediate harm that I'd expected. Instead, with each step, the shape became clearer and I started to see a series of next steps emerge from the mist. I began to see the bones of the ghost and then the flesh. As I saw its structure, I also saw its weaknesses and flaws. It stopped being quite so terrifying. As I got to know it better, I realised it was part of me. I'd created it, and as such it held all my deepest secrets. If I wanted to accept and understand myself better it was the obvious thing to get to know. My new pal even followed me around. The truth was that I couldn't even go on holiday without it coming with me.

I also realised that this fear thing was far from just an academic interest. Some years before I started any enquiry into the subject, I'd chosen to leave my last 'job'. This was a thing I'd put off for years, and I'd only finally done it because I'd reached a tipping point in the relationship between the forces that I felt kept me secure and those which defined me at a cellular level. In my years of working for others I had walked a long way away from the person I really was. The strain had become stressful and something had to break. I had a photograph of myself at five years old and, as I looked at it, I knew I'd lost the spark that child held. My own cheeky face spoke to me and, whenever I looked at it, I felt the need to re-engage with the pre-school possibility of who I really was.

The challenge was that I wasn't capable of honouring this without starting the long walk towards my own deepest fears. When I left my job, this is what I'd finally done. By the time I started to work on fear some years later, I'd been working on this in myself for a good few years. I now had a business that I'd slowly built up, largely through walking hand in hand with my own fears. Although this seems obvious now, I didn't initially connect my own challenges with my general interest in fear. But as I started to see how fear showed up for others I increasingly felt happy to throw my own experiences into the mix, and as time went on I felt happier to talk about what I'd found. My reticence to speak about my personal experience melted away as I saw the parallels with what others were experiencing. I was doing this because it mattered to me. Not only that, I was here not because I knew anything particular that others didn't, but because I was myself struggling through similar challenges.

'Fear' is first and foremost a word, a label for a bunch of things that fall within its broad church. As we start to hack our own, one conversation we logically ought to have is: what do we mean by fear? I've always been wary of this; as an example, one of the things I did in the materials for our early experiments was to include a warning that we didn't intend to address phobias such as fear of spiders or flying. My attitude to this has changed, however. This is because I've seen a number of situations where these obvious surface fears have been connected to a deeper underlying fear. In practice, having a clear phobia has helped people to hack the original source of their fear because it has given them something more solid to get hold of, which provides a route into the deeper well that sits darkly below.

I'm therefore now more inclined to be open to what qualifies as fear than to try to limit it. Fear can show up in everything from standing up in a room to speak to the deepest conversations about life and death. It occurs to a young girl standing at the shore, worried about her first adventure, just as it plays on the mind of the elderly gent in secure retirement, facing the uncertainty of his final years. What I mean when I talk about fear in this book is anything that resides in the mind that is not justified by solid evidence. If you are walking down the high street and crazed madman with a gun is coming the other way, you would be wise to take knowledge of what might happen seriously and respond appropriately. In this situation, our reaction to the clear and present risk is quick and practical. Our feelings in the presence of danger have a role, and the purpose of this book isn't to question that role.

In the Fear Hack work I've done, and in this book, fear is everything else that exists as a story that we make up. It may feel real, but do we have evidence that the thing we fear happening is actually happening now? This includes fears that we self-create, but it also includes those that are created by others which end up controlling us. Fear, in all its colours, whether it is at work or at play, outdoors or indoors, wherever it exists in our lives, is worth having a conversation about. By talking about it we will find out more about what it really is and where it gets its energy from.

This is also a question of qualification. When does this stray into the things that only trained psychologists should be allowed to deal with? This is something that I have worried about and I continue to be conscious of. However, one evening I was invited to do a Fear Hack workshop with a group of psychologists, upstairs in a pub in London. This group gets together regularly to discuss the latest developments in their field in a relaxed and open manner. As the drinks started to flow, I wondered how royally my conversation about fear would be torn apart by these brilliant minds. The ravaging ghost of Freud never appeared, however. The evening turned out to be one of the best I have ever had. What I realised is that these people, just like many of us, do what they do because they have a personal interest in and need for it. All they wanted to do was the same as everyone else. They wanted to talk about what troubled them. In short, I saw that the psychologists were as nuts as we all are, and that what we all need more than anything is to discuss our fears in a supportive environment. I am now deeply suspicious of anything that stands in the way of an encouragement for us all to talk more.

This book isn't just about fear, though. It is about how we approach the subject differently. Specifically, the 'hack' in the title is about how we turn the subject around in order to come at it from another direction entirely. It's always important to do the work itself, but if we are chopping wood, our finest work doesn't just come from raw sweaty blows made repeatedly in the same place. Every so often, we'll benefit from looking at what we are doing, particularly if we are struggling. If we can turn the log around and thereby find an opening that requires only the gentlest of knocks, why wouldn't we choose that way? There is something here of Einstein's idea of only being able to solve a problem by working at a different level from that at which it was created. With fear, my breakthrough didn't come easily, however, and in the end, it took an experience with a dinosaur on a bus to help me to think about fear differently.

The gift came from my habit of heading straight for the top deck on a double-decker bus. The childish pleasure of sitting at the front, effectively in the driver's seat, but one storey up, is too much to resist. From here, it is not only the luxury of being driven that I revel in, it is also the joy of having one of the best views in London. This particular time, however, it wasn't to be. I could see that there was a toy dinosaur sitting in my seat, with a small boy and his mother sitting opposite. The bus was also busy. At the top of the stairs, I turned left into the crowded middle section of the top floor and, in a wobbly crouch as the bus moved forward, walked down the bus to take the first empty double seat behind several outcrops of people. As I settled down, I did what I always love doing on buses: I watched and listened.

It immediately became apparent that everyone was talking about the dinosaur. This surprised me. Firstly, the dinosaur wasn't really that big. It sat comfortably on its seat, with only its head and neck popping up in view for us to see, like some bus Nessie. Secondly, it was a child's blow-up plastic toy; hardly anything surprising. As I listened in to what the couple opposite me and then the people in front of me were saying, I realised the dinosaur had tickled their imaginations. The dinosaur had been received into their lives like a treasure that sparked not only a conversation but also a change in mood.

In the days that followed, the dinosaur stayed with me, and I became interested in the idea of what caused everyone to talk about it. Why, I wondered, does nobody want to talk about the elephant in the room, and yet everyone was talking about the dinosaur on the bus? It took a little while, but eventually I saw something I'd missed.

What I'd failed to notice was the bus. What the dinosaur had done was to draw my attention to this crucial but unspoken other dynamic; the bus and the room that framed the action in both cases. Suddenly I saw that my enquiry was all about the bit of the equation – bus or room – that nobody was talking about. The problem with the original elephant is not so much the object itself but the framework, the room, which contains it. Much as we tend to focus on an object, the lens through which we see the object is critically important to how we see that object. The object can even become a distraction. How often have we all focused on the elephant that no one wants to talk about and, as a result, not had any meaningful conversation about the culture, perspective or the assumptions surrounding it – the 'room' within which the issue itself is contained?

Aldous Huxley famously captured an insight that had already been made by others including psychologist William James and philosophers Henri Bergson and Ferdinand Schiller. In his book about his trip on mescaline, *The Doors of Perception*, Huxley talked of our brain being a 'reducing valve'. Our mind cannot possibly cope with everything, so it selects a 'measly trickle', as Huxley put it, from the whole. What is more, we are blind to much of what sits in its framing of that selection. Some of this blindness is held by each of us individually, but much is held and reinforced collectively. Just as a fish cannot see the water that surrounds it, our view of anything is limited by the frame that we put around it. All we see are clues to that limited frame, not the frame itself. These will often be the things that annoy or surprise us. Just as the odd bubble of air floating upwards could allow a fish to sense that it is in water, sometimes the clues to the framing are hard to notice. It stands to reason that the medium through which we see tends to be invisible to us.

With fear, I realised that same thing was happening. The framework that sits around fear, about which we don't speak, is one of power. Fear is born in a system of power and it thrives in a continuation of this system. For this reason, one of the things Fear Hack does is to focus on not just fear but the system of power, the framework that surrounds it. Essentially, power is the bus that frames the dinosaur of fear. We don't tend to think about that framework, but quietly, out of sight, it influences everything we see. In this framing lies all the things that stop us. If we change the framework and the narrative it spawns, fear can evolve into something that is more useful.

As Fear Hack has developed, the conversations about it and the possibilities of what we could achieve with it have also developed. Their latest evolution is a challenge to the thing we currently call fear. There is a danger that this loosely defined creature of the mind has become bigger than it needs to be. Our fears easily multiply and all too often are used as a tool against us. We are wonderfully adaptable creatures but, as we reach for the stars, we remain fragile. In reality, we are, most of us, in fear of something right now. Some of the genuine dangers we face, such as fire, quake and tempest, need our attention, and most of these won't go away, but the fears of failure and embarrassment that many of us feel in our day-to-day lives are actually fully addressable. On the wider stage, many people in the world are fearful of not having things that are basic human needs – such as food and shelter. These are all fears as well. Similarly, these fears are, if we put our minds to it, also solvable.

Today I want to ask, given the technology and the knowledge we have, whether fear, in the form we have grown up knowing it, is still useful – and if so, how? Does fear now really serve the human race as a whole, and what might we be capable of becoming if we were free from having to be scared?

This starts as an individual possibility for each of us, but it is also a collective one, for us together. If we act to address our collective fears as a species, what then might be possible?

Welcome to Fear Hack.

# 1. Hacking Fear

'You need to get out now!' the man in the street below shouted as he looked up.

This was not what I had expected. Curious, because things had gone quiet, I'd gone to the window, opened it and looked out over the square. Our session was due to start, but the flow of people into the room, marked by the opening of the swing door and the appearance of another apprehensive face, had stopped. This was mirrored down in the square, where, apart from a few policemen and a couple of people moving quickly away in the distance, this usually busy area was now deserted. The sudden absence of people, both here in the room and outside, felt all wrong.

We were in the library of Conway Hall, an events venue on a corner of leafy Red Lion Square near Holborn in central London. The library is secreted away upstairs, up a grand, open staircase almost hidden behind the front entrance. On arrival, we'd all been surprised to see the whole of the lower part of the building laid out end to end with grand pianos. There was a high-end piano auction in London that week and in the middle of the hallway one flamboyant elderly man was midway through a piece, putting a piano through its paces, his hair moving at a different rhythm from his nodding head. It wasn't just a collection of pianos, it was a cacophony of sound, as people tried out their potential purchases. The first thing we'd noticed was that this jarring noise beneath us had ceased.

The serious-looking man below me stood guard, just outside a cordon of police tape. By some magic, he'd managed to tape up the very building that we were inside without telling us. Anyone who approached the area was bounced away at speed. It became obvious that, in the clearing of the building, we'd been overlooked. He seemed momentarily confused by how this had happened as he continued to talk into his radio, commanding what looked like a major operation. One look at him told me that he was not the sort of guy you messed with. He was clearly police, but not of a type that anyone was meant to notice until he decided otherwise. Although he was casually dressed, it looked like his jacket concealed a weapon.

After a short pause, he almost reluctantly delivered his killer blow.

'There's a bomb in the lobby below you,' he shouted out. He definitely had my attention now. It was now clear that we were occupying what had become an isolated island right at the heart of a danger zone. I had no idea what it was meant to feel like to be in the middle of a bomb scare. What I did know is that this didn't feel at all like I might have expected. As well as being a lot to take in, my overriding feeling was that this wasn't meant to happen, here, now, or to me. I had other things I wanted to do.

In the absence of any response, he asked in a slightly surprised voice, 'What are you doing up there?'

I was still in shock; my world, as it had been moments before, had been shattered. 'I'm running a workshop,' I responded, at which I noticed a flicker of irritation cross his face. Did this man think I was an idiot?

'How many of you are there?' he asked.

A quick look around: 'Six,' I replied. He seemed ok with that. At least, whatever else he thought, he now knew we were harmless.

I turned to the others in the room and explained the situation. As I relayed what had happened, things became clearer. If there had ever been a doubt in my mind about what we were going to do, it was now gone. We had to get out, even if it meant walking down through the lobby below us, right past an explosive that could go off at any time. We'd do what we'd been told to do. Taking that risk seemed more expedient than simply waiting here to be blown up by a device right beneath us.

As we followed each other out of the door, past our carefully laid out table of snacks, down the marble stairs into the lobby, past the pianos, out into the street and beyond the tape, it became obvious that we had no idea where we were now going. The bomb had blown up the plan for the workshop and I had no replacement. Somebody suggested we decamp to an upmarket pub on the opposite side of the square. We headed towards the pub, as my mind raced ahead. Realising we had others potentially joining us, I broke off to go back to ask the police what would have happened to the rest of the people who'd tried to get in. We'd had a full house of over 30 booked to come. The answer was obvious. 'We'd have sent them home.' Of course. What else could you say? I got out my phone to send an email to the participants and to answer the messages I now saw had been coming in.

As I joined the group in the pub, drinks were just arriving and I started to move the group towards an empty table in the main room. As our intention became clear, Carol, one of the participants, came up to me to tell me she was not happy sitting there. She explained that if the bomb went off we would be directly in the firing line of shattering glass from the large picture windows overlooking the square. At this moment, I saw that there was a perspective here I wasn't getting. I finally woke up to what was going on in the room. I started to come out of my initial shock. Stuff was happening here and now, in this group, and I hadn't been entirely alive to it.

I asked at the bar if they had any other space and they kindly offered us a room downstairs. Carol was immediately much happier with this plan and, as we led the way downstairs into a snug room I saw that the workshop could live on here, if it so chose. By this route, we had let things find their own natural way forward. It was at this point that I finally saw what had happened as an opportunity rather than the complete disaster it felt. Here I was, running a workshop on fear, suddenly realising that the workshop had already started – just not in the way I had planned. Fear had used a different doorway to enter. My own fears had distracted me from noticing it.

Fear Hack started as, and remains at its core, a workshop and a conversation. It started one Friday afternoon in a basement space on Neal Street in London's Covent Garden at an event called 'The Lab', where anyone who attends can bring an experiment they haven't tried before, to try it out. Of all the things we did that day, one simple thing touched me. In this exercise, we were encouraged to sit for a moment in pairs and to think quietly about our fears. We then wrote a fear down on a card and shared this with our partner, who in turn was encouraged to offer their support to us. We then swapped over.

The exercise brought a moment of quiet introspection as I sat thinking about what my fears were, followed by a moment of intimacy as I shared what I'd chosen with my partner. I remember the person I'd chosen to work with leaning towards me, putting their hand on my arm, looking directly at me, and telling me, 'Don't worry, it'll be ok.'

Somehow this simple statement, delivered by a relative stranger in such an intimate way, did something I wouldn't have expected. The sharing of the fear but, perhaps most memorably, the unconditional support that I got when I did, fundamentally shifted my relationship with my fear. I started to see fear not as a lurking demon that visited me from time to time when it chose, but more as something I could sit down with and talk to constructively. Being so close to it helped. That was the moment I decided there was something here that I needed to explore further.

When I left the Lab, it was this supportive move from another person that stayed with me. The unexpected motion of caring continued to be present and had an effect on me which made no rational sense. The feeling that I got in that moment has stayed with me to this day. I'd never looked at fear from a kind and positive perspective before. I felt a mood shift, and that shift contained a gift I wanted to keep. I went away that day not just with a new interest in fear but also a philosophy of how I wanted to develop that interest. I described it as making fear my friend. I didn't yet understand why, but I knew that if I turned my relationship with fear into a friendship, it would show me things about myself that I would benefit from knowing.

In the weeks that followed my interest deepened. I decided to reach out to the people closest to me and to ask them what they thought about fear. I got some great suggestions and did a lot of reading. At one point a psychologist I spoke to recommended I watch Chris Hadfield's TED talk. Hadfield is an engineer and former fighter pilot who was the first Canadian to walk in space. He served on two space shuttle missions and was the commander of the International Space Station, though he is perhaps best known for his rendition of David Bowie's 'Space Oddity', played on his guitar whilst in orbit.

Given his line of work, Hadfield is certainly qualified to talk about fear. In his TED talk, he starts by asking us, what is the scariest thing we have ever done? He then quickly asks another question: what is the most *dangerous* thing you have ever done? For Hadfield, we know the answer is likely to involve space, where the risk of catastrophe is high. In the early shuttle launches it was one in nine – better than the one in six of Russian Roulette, but still not great. Even in Hadfield's time it was one in 38. In these sorts of environments, the players have to manage their risk. The astronaut thus learns to test for what might go wrong. Simulations – 'the sim' – are a key part of the training. If your job involves being strapped into a chair and thrust into space with a bunch of rockets going off below you, it stands to reason that you might want to prepare yourself for all the things that might go wrong. In the sim you'll learn things that could save your life. These same things will also help to assuage your fears as you sit there, wait-ing for lift-off. If you've tested for all the things that might go wrong you are likely to feel a whole lot better about your chances. As Had-field says in his book *An Astronaut's Guide to Life on Earth,* he learned to 'sweat the small stuff'.

I found the substance of Hadfield's message instantly appealing. His approach is to tell us the logic. He points out that the vast majority of spiders will not bite us, and that we can just walk into spider webs. This is a strategy we can apply to anything, and by this route we can conquer our fear, just as he has. This approach to fear undoubtedly works, and the idea that we should face our fears and walk directly through them is not new. The idea, born in the rational world, that we should 'fear not', knowing that our fears will crumble once we take them on, is a good one.

I got this, but I now also saw a good reason why Hadfield's opening change in question had piqued my curiosity. He was talking much more about danger than he was about fear. The two overlap and are interconnected, but danger is more external, factual and calculable. If we manage danger and risk it helps ease our fear, but these external realities are not the same thing as our internal, mind-forged imag-inaries. NASA is, quite correctly, in the business of managing risk, but I am far more interested in fear. Fear exists in our minds and logic struggles to touch it. It is different to danger, which exists in the moment and, like pain, is what actually happens. Fear is internal to us and more shadowy. As such, it is more difficult to pin down. It is difficult to walk into a thing that we are struggling to put a shape to. I was increasingly seeing that the first part of my job was to give form to something that drew part of its power from being indistinct.

I also knew there was more to making fear our friend than simply walking up to it and taking it on. Much as this appealed to me, I knew I for one failed to do it on a regular basis. As I worked more with fear I saw that this was true for others also. There were a lot of people for whom the 'just take it on' approach simply didn't work in everyday life. It was too confrontational. It was much easier to avoid what felt too much like a battle. Indeed, why was it necessary at all? Much as we applaud the notion of bravely facing everything we fear, the fact remains that many of us, sitting alone inside our houses, are still scared to go out.

At the same time, I realised I was falling into a trap. This interest in fear was about more than just knowing. The problem with my doing a lot of reading and research is that it can play to my desire to master a topic and to become an 'expert' at it. I recognised that I found it too easy to become insular, self-reliant and turned in. In my gut, I knew that if I was going to really make friends with fear as I wanted to, I had to do the opposite of what I'd become comfortable with; instead of turning in, I had to turn outward to others. To do that I had to befriend one of my own fears first – namely the vulnerability I felt about setting up a workshop involving other people. I knew that rather than just thinking about fear, I needed to do some experiments and to try some ideas out. I had to *feel* stuff rather than think it. My own fears warned against this ceding of control but I knew this work had to be done in a group setting where the work was set in a relational context, not just a rational one. If this scared me too, all the better.

One day I got talking to a friend, Alison Sayers, about these ideas, and together we hatched a plan. I had got to know Alison when she'd led learning and development in a consultancy. She'd since left and was now training as a teacher in the Grinberg Method, which focused on learning through the body. Alison wanted to explore fear as it showed up physically, so we agreed to put on our own experiment and to invite people to it. Within a few days I'd found a venue and had set up a web page to advertise the event. Suddenly this was happening. To me what we were doing had a supportive 'club' feel to it, so as we'd chosen a Friday afternoon to run it we decided to call it 'Friday Club'. All we needed was a few people for it to work. Our feeling was that whoever turned up and whatever happened would be exactly what we needed. Our job was to respond to the opportunity.

Contrary to my fears, people did turn up to Friday Club. We ran the experiment four times, changing it and refining it as we went. By the fourth running, things had changed; Alison was moving out of London to concentrate on other things and I was struggling with the constraints of the original idea. It felt right to end the experiment. After the workshop, I told the group about this decision. It was only then, sitting in a circle on a polished parquet floor, at the end of the last Friday Club, that the participants told me what they really thought. I didn't want to listen because my mind was made up, but for once I couldn't escape.

The group said that there was a power in what we were doing and a feeling that that power was only just starting to emerge. They said, in no uncertain terms, that I had to stick with it. I went away still determined to kill it, but something about it wouldn't go away. A couple of months later I stopped resisting and decided to rebirth the idea. This time was different though. The Friday Club experiment had provided a loose foundation, but this was now about building something more distinct upon that base. I was now committed to it being about fear. I also wanted to challenge myself and others to call out that this was about tackling fear differently. There was no point to this if there wasn't a reinvention.

In this space, 'Fear Hack' was born. This shift allowed me to do the exercises we found worked best with even more confidence, under a clearer theme, with more energy. The workshop got simpler but also more conversational. Sometimes, it is only when you are prepared to walk away from something that you can see it for what it wants to be as opposed to what we might want from it. When we are open to what the world is asking for, things start to happen.

Now, the first exercise we do in the workshops is to get a bunch of still slightly reluctant people to identify what their biggest fear is. We ask them, if they are happy, to describe that fear in a few words on a Post-It note that they can stick on the wall with everyone else's. At least one person always asks if they can put more than one fear up and I am happy to embrace the promise that lies behind their question and the emerging sense of willingness in the group by saying yes. The creation of this 'Fear Wall' is an absurdly simple exercise, yet it always delivers a moment of depth and power that stays with the group throughout the rest of the workshop.

The wall is soon a multicoloured patchwork of small pieces of paper, each with some small words on. What they represent is something far bigger. Each tiny piece of paper on the large expanse of wall carries a message that comes right from the heart of the individual who has had the courage to write those few words down. These words acknowledge that fear restricts life; that it constricts what we might otherwise have. It also says that we feel its effects even if we don't often talk about it. When we come together to do this, we have started the process of noticing not just our fear but its effect on our behaviour. We are accepting that we are ready to talk about what is going on.

This noticing happens on an individual level, but now it is also the start of something collective. Some of the group will go up to the wall, stick their note up and walk away; task done. This moving away from the wall is a thing to notice also. It's important that the people who have walked away with their own thoughts come back and look, to gather around the thing that this group has created together. As people stand in a polite arc before the wall, I ask them how they feel. It is never long before someone talks about their surprise in seeing something they have not seen before. Suddenly they are faced with what everyone else's fear means to them. Most have never thought, let alone known, what others are feeling until now. One of the unspoken truths for many is there are other people here that they are wary of or that they find slightly scary. What they now see is that even those people have fears. There is no 'us and them'; we are all in this together. Someone will mention this and say that the notes tell them that they are not alone. For the first time, we see that other people, whoever they are, have fears similar to our own.

Someone else will then point out that many of the fears are shared. Often, the group will start to explore connections and themes. At this point, many of the group will be looking around in wonder, amazed that they have not thought to ask, compare fears or seek the support of others before now. A realisation sinks in that although our fears feel like things that run around inside our own heads, they are also a shared thing that connects us. There is a conversation to be had that we are not yet having. We can help each other.

Fear Hack follows this theme. What we are doing is saying that we are no longer content with a model that separates us, either from each other or from our fears. We are no longer going to accept an approach that results in us being at the behest of something we don't really understand. We don't want to unwittingly run away or feel that we have to be in confrontation with our fears. We want to understand them, because we've realised that with understanding things can change for the better, often in ways that we can't yet foresee.

As it turned out, the suspected bomb underneath our workshop that evening did not go off. There was no Conway Hall piano bomber after all, because there was no bomb. Our fears are like that bomb. They exist in our minds as a construct that feels real, even though there is nothing really there. They can be constructed out of thin air. Our thoughts are just thoughts. What is more, our fears can birth in as little as a moment's suspicion or a misunderstanding. And while there are common themes, each fear we have goes on to affect each of us differently. Carol's fear about the window was something that was present for her but not, before they heard it, for others. Each of us was affected differently by the nonexistent bomb that night. Fear is a construct of the mind reacting to circumstances. It is its own suspect device. Fear Hack seeks to challenge this. Both here and in our workshops, but perhaps most importantly as a tool for everyday situations, it asks the mind if it is prepared to start to question itself. This is a process whereby we accept that the mind *can* change, and then ask it whether it is ready to do so.

As I've looked more deeply into what fear is, the thing that has continued to surprise me is how deeply it has its claws stuck into us. We might think that our daily anxieties are a thing we can understand and manage on a logical level, but the problem is that the quick-fix solutions don't go anywhere near the root. As we start to understand how fear restricts us, we also see how it invades our everyday behaviour and becomes part of who we are. It is used as a tool to control our behaviour, but it also operates at a deeper level. We learn to respond to fear in a particular way because we feel that response protects us at the time. We then cling to, defend and repeat that strategy. A repeated behaviour becomes an instinctive habit. By this method, our response to fear cleverly and silently becomes part of our belief systems and our identity.

As the scare hit us I saw something of this in myself as my character reacted in its own way. On that night in Conway Hall, I already had my own embedded behaviours, and these conditioned how I responded to what happened. As the events of the evening unfolded, I prioritised according to these. Someone who had watched me in the past may well have been able to predict how I would react. With a workshop to run and my own narrative about what I thought should happen, I was contained by both my own expectations and my own habitual strategies. For a while, I was unable to appreciate the situation fully or to tune in to what was really going on. This limited me and is why, for me, engaging with fear at the theoretical level was no longer enough. And this is why our actual reactions to the 'bombs' in our lives are so important. These incidents, as they happen, are our gateway to understanding how fear shapes us at the core of who we are. Fear Hack thus also looks at how what scares us makes us. We create strategies in response to our fears. The good news is that they are only strategies. They are not who we are. These strategies are something we can change, if we want to.

The cold reality though, is that change is hard. It's hard because ultimately it doesn't happen afterwards, in quiet reflection. It only ever really happens on the field of play, in the moment. Change happens in our on-the-spot adaption and on-the-job learning in response to the changing events we are faced with. To do this requires us to keep going. It requires us not to be stopped by our fears.

That night, things kept changing, and after the bomb squad had arrived and defused the supermarket shopping bag that did not, as it turned out, contain a bomb, we were allowed to reassemble in the same spot we'd had to abandon an hour or so before. Quietly, I was grateful, not so much for the opportunity to go back but more for the additional challenge this further change brought. I felt I'd learned something from my slow reaction earlier and felt that all of us had more to learn that night, if only we stuck at it. This included warmly welcoming all the offers this strange night was bringing us.

As we all walked back in, it felt a little like an abandoned city after a disaster. Not only had the piano players been scared into silence, the safe shared space we'd endeavoured to create had gone. We were all closer for having spent some time together, but the shadow of the bomb still pervaded the mood; it had disrupted the feeling of safety we had started to create. Now, back in the room, much as I felt a sense of loss of what we had, I knew we had to work with what had happened: here we were, sitting back down in the same chairs to talk about our own deepest fears, with a very real experience of fear already in our midst. Instead of simply picking up from where we'd left off, I started by asking everyone talk about their experiences of the last hour. During that conversation, the mood shifted and the safe space returned. That evening we ended up having some of the frankest conversations about fear that I've ever had.

In every workshop I've ever held I've always been aware of the need to create a feeling of safety. It probably comes from my background in negotiation, when frequently heightened tempers first need to be calmed and then understood. I realised by trial and error that unless a person feels safe nothing truly revealing will happen. A person who feels safe behaves fundamentally differently.

It is therefore this feeling of safety itself that I want to explore first. It is the gateway to how we change the way that we engage with fear. The simple fact is that we do stuff when we feel safe that we'd never do when we feel more anxious. So, first we are going to explore what this means. What is the secret of the hand on the arm, the sharing, and the calm we feel in this safe space, and how do we achieve it? In the next chapter we'll ask: how could simply being in this state help to transform our relationship with fear?

Below is a selection from Fear Walls created in Fear Hack workshops.

Being found out
Failing
Rejection
Not having enough money
Poor health
Mental decline
Not being able to support family
Not being loved for who I am
Not being wanted
Found to be wrong
Loneliness
Getting bored
Not doing anything important with my life
Being alone
Not getting approval
Ageing
Not getting what I want
Ridicule
Family getting hurt
Being abandoned
Losing what I have
Being mediocre
Not enough work

Environmental apocalypse
Losing my job
The judgement of others
Not living up to my potential
Being trapped
Letting people down
Not being good enough
Being a bad parent/family member
Running out of time
Suffering in pain or with illness
Getting old
Being humiliated
Falling short of expectations
Repeating the mistakes of my parents
Success itself
Not having enough
I've left it too late
Not finishing
Not having it in me
Not enjoying life enough
Not being included
The unknown
All the above*

(* yes, this final observation was added underneath a sea of fears)

What do you notice?

# 2. Red, Amber, Green

Garrett Morgan was born in Kentucky in 1877. His parents had both been slaves and Morgan worked most of his teenage years as a handyman. In his late teens, he moved to the town of Cleveland in search of opportunity. Once there, Morgan became an expert at repairing sewing machines, opened his own shop and, in time, started to fix anything else that needed repairing. As Morgan got to know more about the inner workings of the world's devices he learned to invent things himself. As a man of African origin, he struggled to get people to take him seriously in early 20th-century America, sometimes even hiring white actors to represent him. He was not a man who allowed difficulty to stop him, however, and eventually he shot to minor fame after a 1916 tunnel explosion under Lake Erie. Morgan, who had invented a breathing hood for use in smoke-filled environments, was able to save several lives. The patented hood he invented went on to become the model for many modern breathing devices.

Sometime around the early 1920s Morgan witnessed an accident between an automobile and a horse-drawn carriage at a busy road intersection in Cleveland. Morgan, unusually for his time and particularly given his challenges in a white-dominated country, owned a motor car, so he understood the driver's perspective. He realised that the problem with early signalling in towns was that they consisted of only two states: stop and go. This was entirely logical, but in practice there was a problem. People had no time to react. What Morgan saw was that something else was needed. He identified that the system was missing a transitionary middle state that warned when things were about to change one way or another. And so the idea of the amber or yellow phase of the modern traffic light was born.

The official record tells us that the traffic light was also invented in a number of other places at about the same time, including by police officer William Potts in nearby Detroit. The same pattern emerges. Potts realised that it was difficult for police officers at four different lights to all change the signal at precisely the same time. On the big junctions in a city it was impossible for any system to cope with real-life traffic without a middle warning stage. Change was coming; Morgan's three-phase invention was granted a patent in 1923 which he subsequently sold to General Electric for $40,000. Given Morgan's difficulties getting acknowledged in those days I'm glad to grant him the recognition I'm sure he deserved for cracking this particular problem.

When I first learned about emotions, I was immediately interested in the idea put forward by psychologists that there are two ways in which we react to events. Apparently, we either move 'towards' or 'away' from whatever happens. Indeed, the root of the word 'emotion' is based on the latin *movēre* – to move. The idea that we tend to react to things as e-motionally one way or another made instinctive sense. I also particularly liked the explanation that we tend to run away from something but only slowly walk towards it. This is borne out by analysis of our basic emotions by people like Professor Paul Ekman. Ekman famously studied indigenous peoples in many parts of the world, looking for common facial expressions and emotions. What he found was that some of these were consistent and universal. His shock finding in the 1970s was that most of the basic emotions we have are negative. We tend to be led by Fear, Disgust, Anger, Sadness and Surprise. According to Ekman these five basic negative emotions outweigh the one positive one: Joy. In a world full of risk and danger that makes sense, as social engagement can be low on our list of priorities. Food and love may be important to us, but the preservation of life itself is far more pressing. If we miss a predator that's about to grab us (fear) or we eat something that poisons us (disgust), we won't be around for the next meal, let alone to cuddle up. Our ancient system prioritises our preservation with an instinctively embedded strategy. We naturally tend to be defensive.

What frankly never made sense to me was that this was a simple linear model which resulted in a movement either one way or the other, like some sort of angry/happy pendulum. I knew that we didn't just go from running away from something in fear of our lives to wanting to engage with it; it wasn't this easy. If we are in a state of fear it takes us a while to even start to feel relaxed. There is a kind of transition zone required, just like the slow phasing between stop and go of the traffic light. When I started to look at this in a bit more detail I came across one theory that immediately made sense: the 'polyvagal theory' put forward by professor of psychiatry Stephen Porges. Porges essentially describes the human nervous system as a kind of governing traffic light with three main phases. Each of the three phases represents a broad zone that our systems might find themselves in: red for freeze (or stop), amber for fight/flight (warning zone) and green for genuine trusting friendship and social engagement (or go).

This system respects the transition zone that we know we need. In a traffic light model, there is no sudden flip from 'away' to 'towards'. If you are in the middle state, amber, you don't want to engage in a nice way. Your system is ready to fight or to run. To want to engage socially, we need to feel comfortable first. Our nervous system has to tell us that we feel safe in order for us to want to move towards anything. If we are fidgety in fight/flight amber, we don't go straight to wanting to hug someone. First we have to move from amber into the friendly, safe green state. Effectively, there are two things going on here: state (how we feel, up and down, the traffic light) and motion (how we respond, forward and back). State and motion work together and, crucially, our state governs us. This means that we only feel like engaging once we feel safe. What this primacy of state also tells us is that there is a crucial difference between towards in amber (fight) and towards in green (safe engagement and love). Essentially, we need this green light before we approach anything in a welcoming frame of mind.

What Porges says is that we are on an evolutionary journey. In humans we don't see the red or freeze state that much any more because we have largely evolved away from any need for it. It is the ancient response of the deep lizard brain that protects the animal by simply freezing as if dead. It is now only in extreme terror that humans tend to exhibit this state. We can find ourselves at times moving towards a freeze response, and we even hear of people losing control of basic functions, such as their bowels, in extremis. So, freeze still shadows us at the top of our nervous system traffic light system, and sometimes we can find ourselves affected by it; some of us more than others. It is what is happening when we freeze up in front of an audience, terrified, unable to speak or do anything. This is different to the 'flight' response, although it's easy to confuse the two. In flight, we want to get out, to run out of the room, while in freeze, we find ourselves seizing up, stopped, unable to move. This is much more likely to be seen in animals that have been around a lot longer than humans, such as birds, which after all are the survivors of dinosaurs. This tends to make sense of the advice some of us were given as kids not to scare an infant chick that has fallen out of its nest, lest it freezes rigid and dies.

What we do see all around us in humans is lots of amber. This is the 'not sure' state. Here we are on constant alert between fight or flight. Do we engage in conflict or do we get out? What Porges says is that the nervous system, mediated by the vagus nerve which runs from our brain stem down our spine to our colon, is on constant alert, monitoring our external environment, deciding for us what state we should be in. The system is constantly making small adjustments to take us up or down the three zones of the main scale. When it is not sure, it puts us in this middle state. If we are not feeling safe we are likely to be here, in a constant state of readiness. This is our fight/flight zone, where we are constantly on edge, not sure whether we should be taking up a battle or getting the hell out of a danger zone.

The green zone of the traffic light is our safe-to-engage state. When we are here our heart rate falls and our body systems start to relax. We have less need to feel defensive and our senses are more open to the world around us. We even see more, because our first priority shifts from a defensive mode, focused on the threat, to a wider appreciation of all that is around us. Porges even explains why the sharing of food tends to put us in this state. It appears that in infancy we rely on food as our primary connection. As we get older, out of the first six months of life, we start to move our response to more social signals. Some semblance of this link between food and safe state remains, which we acknowledge when we break bread together and make drinks for each other. Food and friendship go together, and they exist in a fundamentally different state from fight and flight. This safe 'friend' state is where we feel most relaxed and creative. It is the state we need to be in to grow, after all. We all have a place where we relax

– for example, many experience a calm, creative feeling whilst in the bath or shower; a place of ultimate relaxation. That is perhaps why the shower scene in the film *Psycho* is so shocking, as unexpected terror invades a place we instinctively expected to be safe.

One of the first things I do on a Fear Hack is to ask people what they'd like to get out of the session. It often becomes clear that there are two different categories of fear. The first is a fear of something that exists in our future. We might worry about an upcoming event or our ability to cope in a particular situation. Fear of this type is what stops us sleeping as we worry ourselves sick about what might be. It is essentially anxiety. (This is something we will talk about later, in Chapter 7.) The other form is a fear in the moment: we struggle when it comes to the event itself. For example, we might know that our issue is getting on our feet to present. We are fine until that point, but it's our reaction when we stand up and see the room that stalls us. Often when we discuss this, people even talk about freezing up. When it happens, this panicked reaction is alarming and even produces its own fear of recurrence. The good news is that this kind of fear, the one that tends to affect us in the moment itself, is something we can start to manage if we start to understand and work with our own traffic light system.

The truth is that although I present and speak quite a lot now, I was someone who avoided it assiduously until my early 30s. I still remember having to stand up at a group meeting at work to tell the rest of the group what I was doing. My heart was racing and I forgot most of what I wanted to say. I am fundamentally an introvert, and I hated it. My big challenge came when my brother asked me to be his best man. Nobody realised, but I was terrified. I worked hard on a speech, under the pressure one has in that situation to be funny. When the day came I gave the speech and it went well. People reacted kindly, but what I will always remember was my father coming up to me afterwards and saying that he didn't know how I'd managed to do it. He shared with me that day that he'd managed to avoid public speaking for his entire career as he'd also been terrified of it. In that moment, my heart went out to him as I realised more deeply both what was going on for him and the importance of the challenge I'd just undertaken and come through. It was only by doing this that I'd gained confidence and broken a barrier that was entirely self-imposed. In the years that followed I did more and more public speaking and started to get a lot more comfortable with it. That comfort came from two things: doing more of it, but also starting to proactively manage my own nervous system using the traffic light idea.

The first time I ever fully worked with the traffic light system and observed it at work was the first time I did a keynote warm-up speech to a large audience. I did it because I started out terrified. The gig wasn't something I'd sought out – I'd just published my first book and been invited for drinks with a CEO contact in a Soho club who was interested in talking about how we might work together. My book – *The Power of Soft* – was about how we can get what we want without being a \*\*\*\*. As I sipped at my drink I slowly realised that the book was simply an entrée to a series of opportunities to talk about the topic of relationships. It also became clear that the CEO's organisation had a conference coming up and were looking for a way to kick off a discussion about what they saw as the 'softer' skills. Because of my book, they assumed that I did this sort of thing all the time. As I heard the bullish 'sales director' part of me bigging up my viewpoint on the topic and my ability to provide a solution, another part of me started to shrink. Before I knew it, I'd not only sold the idea that I could speak at the conference, I'd also pitched a topic for my talk. As the client got increasingly excited about this idea, I felt a desire to back-pedal rapidly build up inside me. I wanted, desperately, to run away.

I wanted to say that I'd never done this before. I wanted to say that I was full of questions as to how I was going to do it. But I also realised that telling the client this wasn't going to help. It felt like a form of respect, not to allow my introvert voice to speak. I realised that the image they had of me had to be kept intact. I'd created an image of myself as the exactly the expert they wanted, and now, however much a part of me was terrified, I had to go with it. My inner voice could so easily undermine the situation, but I just had to ignore it, instead seeing things as others, those I'd sold a vision to, now saw them.

As what I'd just pitched for became clear I slowly breathed in and said that yes, I'd be delighted to do it. Five hundred people, no problem. When were they thinking? I'd see if I was free. I was, and put the date in my diary.

It's always a relief when something is months away, hiding in the diary, yet to reveal itself. Somehow, deep down, our body knows this and quietly prepares itself. Eventually, though, the time comes to do something real and tangible, like make some notes. In the build-up to the day there was lots of work I did to get myself ready, but the most critical thing I did was not about preparing my talk – it was about shifting how I felt on the day by combining the idea of the traffic light model and what it took to be in the green light zone with what I'd already learned about myself and how I'd started to deal with stress. Over the years I'd got better and better at staying calm in heightened situations. I'd had to do this because I found that I was particularly sensitive to my environment. I couldn't shrug it off like many others seemed to. When I went into a client's big impressive building, I now made sure that I didn't become granite myself. I made an effort to keep my humanity. Instead of clamming up and going into myself, I learned to open up. I had a conversation with anyone I could find. Instead of ignoring the security guard, I'd say hi and ask if he was having a good day. We joke about 'small talk', but it feathers the edges, and over time I realised that it was much less about good manners – I'd started to do it because it made me feel more comfortable. I knew there was a trick here that worked.

I particularly remembered a negotiation I'd been involved in at the head offices of a multinational chemical company in Munich years before. The building had recently been completed at vast expense on one of the best streets in the city. The boss's chauffeur-driven car was parked in its own turning circle outside, and as we went in the entire wall, behind a pair of identically dressed female receptionists, was dominated by a fish tank that extended upwards through the building. The place reeked of power, and as a supplier we had every reason to be on the back foot. Five of us had arrived the night before and had psyched ourselves up for this early start. I had the responsibility for a new client and a new deal resting on my shoulders. A large part of me wanted to run, to not be here at all. Now, even the suited-and-booted good corporate citizen part of me was starting to panic inside, as a sweat developed and my heart rate rose. I knew I had to master this and, introducing the team at the reception desk, I found a better part of myself behaving as humanly as I could. I felt utterly intimidated by the situation but refused to give in to it. Instead, I asked the women behind the power desk how they were today.

I got a good response, so I kept going. What I found was that as we talked about the fish and the history of the building I relaxed and so, slowly, did everyone else. Sensing this, I didn't stop there. When we went upstairs to set up for our meetings, I continued to be curious. I let my inner child ask questions about what I saw rather than defaulting to the sombre mood. The client's nature was to be aggressive, and when they tried this we refused to allow the mood to shift. By lunchtime the lead negotiator for this complex company, who had a reputation for being difficult, was a best friend who took great pride in buying us, his new friends, lunch, during which time we learned much more about the fish. It turned out that, as the head of procurement, he'd had to buy them and wasn't a fan. Fish weren't simple to keep in an office building, it transpired. He then opened up and told us a host of secrets about the building and its extravagant foibles. We learned that his ultimate boss liked show and had demanded the fish as an impressive backdrop to the reception area. The manner of his explaining about the fish and then his relationship with his employer leached into the way he talked to us about the deal itself. None of this would have happened if we had allowed the mood of the building to affect us. We'd managed to take something in with us and to keep it with us. It had worked.

This approach works because we can take active ownership of our own systems. As Stephen Porges explains, our nervous system continually monitors our external environment for threats. In the past, these would have been predators who were out to attack us. Nowadays, it can be anything that we feel is going to threaten us, from a stressful meeting to an unpredictable boss. We still have a system that is built to deal with lions and tigers, even though we no longer need it. The system still looks for big cats about to eat us. The first trick is to realise that the big cats have gone. Threats of imminent death are a rare exception rather than the norm. Although our nervous system might experience a threat as significant, most of the threats we face are not of the same order. As we stand up to present to a room of people, the idea of our failing to make an impression in the room may feel like the possibility of death, but the truth is it is far from it. You have a choice. You don't have to give in to the perceived threat. There is no lion.

What happens is that when our system identifies a threat it puts us in amber, to prepare us for fight/flight. To do this it readies all our senses and raises our heart rate. We start breathing differently; we might perhaps take in more air or, if we move towards red on the scale, we might even stop breathing for a moment as we prepare for the possibility of freezing. Our vision changes and we tend to focus on a limited range of sight ahead of us: tunnel vision. Our hearing can constrict and we might even struggle to hear what is said. If we are now focusing on defending ourselves we are not going to pick up the subtle nuances of what we should have heard. As we move further into amber we essentially close down. We are not as open to the wider world. Our priority is to defend ourselves from the metaphorical lion.

Everyone reacts differently. Some of us are thick skinned and some of us are more sensitive, like Proust perhaps, once described as 'a man born without a skin'. The best comparator is perhaps exercise. We all react differently to exercise. Some are naturally fitter, whilst others have the benefit of training; some take it in their stride, whilst others are panting and out of breath quickly. Either way, the feeling we have after a bit of exercise is similar. If I run for a bit and then stop, the feeling I have, the shortness of breath, is similar to the feeling of being in amber. I can then notice how quickly it subsides and I get back to normal. The same is true of the speed at which our nervous system adjusts. Once on high alert some of us struggle to restabilise, whilst the pulse rate of others returns to normal more quickly. The amount of adrenalin and other chemicals that are naturally released affects us all differently. What is clear is that too much of these stress-related chemicals can be harmful. It's like running an engine on choke, with a high fuel mix; if we do too much of it the engine suffers and can stall. We humans don't tend to burn these fight/flight chemicals up or shake them out of our bodies as well as animals do. Because it's a new area we've got a lot to learn, but we've got better at understanding the benefits of exercise in recent years, and in time we'll hopefully also get better at taking care of our nervous systems. The similarities are obvious once we start exploring them, and I suspect there may be great benefits for our long-term health in taking such care.

This subconscious system explains why even actions that seem small can have a major effect on us. If we are talking to someone and they pick up their mobile phone it can have a devastating effect on how we feel. Something as innocent as someone glancing at their watch to check the time can be picked up by our nervous system as a threat. We can quickly move from the green of friend to the amber of fight. Other people's attention and engagement matters to us, and we monitor these microsystems constantly. Similarly, a few kind words from someone we care about can matter more than anything else in the world, giving us a rosy glow and helping us to feel safe and loved. All these things have an effect, particularly in the more sensitive of us. We may not be monitoring these changes consciously, but our nervous system does. The fact that the nervous system constantly influences our mood under the radar is a problem in one sense, but it is also a route to a cure in another. We can kid the system. Instead of letting it decide what state we are in, we can choose to work with it. We are told it is subconscious, autonomic, out of our control, but that doesn't mean that we can't influence it if we get to understand it.

When I arrived to present to the deeply scary room of 500 people at the request of my CEO friend, I finally got to test this out. As the room slowly filled up with people, what I did was to use experiments with my own nervous system to calm myself. The first thing I did, standing there, was to cut out the internal chatter about what was to come. I prioritised how I *felt* over what I *knew*. I did something I'd thought about but never done properly in a disciplined way before. I put any worries about what I was going to say to one side. I realised that if I started to have any doubts about my content these thoughts would escalate and affect how I felt. If I hadn't prepared well enough, nothing I could do now would fix that.

Saying this was all very well, but I found the real challenge, as ever, lay in the moment itself. There, waiting in the room, the thoughts started to come. Whatever I'd told myself, I wanted to look at the few slides I had. I felt the urge to open my laptop, then to check my phone. These small checks are what we do. There was a point where I found it almost impossible to resist this urge and nearly cracked – but then, instead, I forced myself to get up and to be open to the room, present to what was happening right there and then. As I waited off to one side of the auditorium, a few attendees started to come in. To make sure I remained present, I stepped forward to talk to one of these early arrivals. I let my green zone 'friend' lead, stopping my amber 'fight' state from taking over. I got a smile and I felt better, which led me to another person and another table. Disciplining myself like this was hard, but I knew I had to give all of my concentration to what was happening in the room now, not to what might come.

The next thing I did was to focus on my breathing. If my system is allowed to drift into amber what it does is to prepare me for fight, flight or even freeze. This affects my breathing. I might even stop breathing. I can either accept this or I can use the system itself to tell my body that things are actually ok. By making sure that I take long, deep breaths, particularly a good long outbreath, my system gets the message that things are safe. It's slightly crafty but it does the job of convincing my nervous system that I'm in the green zone. If ever I feel tense or nervous now I go to my breathing first. It almost seems so obvious that doing it doesn't seem necessary, and yet every time I make the effort to do it consciously, it helps.

Then I opened my other senses. To do this, I listen to the room and notice the sounds. If I can, I look out of the window and see what is going on outside. Suddenly a pecking bird or a tree waving in the wind provides a stabilising force. As someone comes in my direction, instead of avoiding them, I step forward, introduce myself and welcome them. This social opening itself calms me. It feels like the last thing I want to do, but moving towards the thing that my senses tells me is a threat has the opposite effect. My senses get the friend support they need. The more I embrace the audience and the room, the better I feel. This continues to work when I start the presentation. The more I engage and ask questions and the more I get a response, the better

I feel. If I love them, they tend to love me back. It's the opposite of what fear would have me do, but it works.

As I stepped forward to welcome people in I also stepped into a different way of thinking about everything that had previously stopped me. This is the realisation that fear feels different in green than it does in amber. In amber, fear is the lion. It is a large predatory thing that is out to get us. We may be indoors, but it rises up and pins us against the wall. Once we are there our options are limited. The lion is big and scary and we are small and weak. The beast is out to get us. It towers over us as we raise our hands up over our heads to protect ourselves from it. All we can do, if we stay here, is to fight it. We might win the fight or we might not. All too often, we run away from it.

Once we are in safe green, fear feels entirely different. It becomes something we can approach. Just like with anything else in our lives, once we feel safe, we feel able to engage. As we relax, we get more open and more creative. It is the same fear, but now we can see it for what it is – it is not the lion that our system would have it be. We are suddenly more resourceful and more flexible. If we walk calmly towards it, fear is different. It is more approachable. It's not some huge monster bearing down upon us. This is the trick. If we let it, our mind will make monsters out of anything. Once we realise that it is our mind and our protective nervous system that is doing this, we can choose to change our approach.

Now, this is all very well, but the danger here is that I am starting to go back on my own promise. In the beginning of this book I said that I'd try not to stand too long in the stream of exhortation of how to live a better life. At this point we have probably already got a little wet. What I said was that I was much more interested in understanding why we don't do what we know we should, and exposing what stops us. In order to go forward with conviction, we need to know what pulls us back. For this reason, we are going to spend the next few chapters looking at how fear has got us into a situation in which living in an anxious amber state, constantly looking for monsters, is too easily the norm. If we can see how fear became such a big issue in the first place it is much easier for us all to make the shift we choose.

We know that the safe green zone gives us everything we need for engagement, joy and creativity. When we are there, we can all see, like John Lennon did, that love is the answer.

But what is it that makes staying there so damn hard?

Where do you feel at your most calm?
And your least?

# 3. The Evolution of Fear

The first thing I knew was that the sky behind me was full of blue flashing lights. The shock of it started a move back into consciousness. I came out of the trance I had been in since coming home from work, stuck in my head, consumed by my own thoughts. The first question was the blue lights. How long had they been flashing, and where were they coming from? It wasn't long before I started to accept something I knew already. The lights were directly behind me, and they weren't moving away. They could only be for me. What had happened was now clear, even if the shock of taking it in was only starting to settle. As I snapped into being more present to what was happening, a different part of me took control of the steering wheel. In my first properly rational act in this new scene, I looked for somewhere to pull over.

A wash of failure raced through me as I stopped and watched the police vehicle pull into the lay-by behind. My pulse was racing, trapped in its own version of how time should pass. I thought about what I should do and whether I should get out of the car. Then I realised that getting out was not what you did. I watched as one of the policemen, slowly and with infuriating deliberation, opened his door and got out of his car. The officer paused again to adjust himself and then, as I lowered my window, slowly, step by step, walked towards my car. It felt wrong not to get out to greet him, but I'd watched enough cop movies to see myself, sitting there in a car, in the film of someone else's life, and know how I had to behave now.

I had got myself into this situation because I was operating on autopilot, not thinking about what I was doing. I'd come home from work, realised I had no groceries in the house and got in the car to pay a visit to the local supermarket. I'd had one of those days at work where nothing had gone right and it seemed that everything and everybody was against me. I was unable to accept anything and was taking it personally. Now it seemed I couldn't even sort out my own food. On the way back from doing my shopping, I was still angry and found myself racing round Lewisham and then the vast open area on

Blackheath in south-east London, burning into the corners like some sort of boy racer with a point to prove.

As the policeman settled at the side of my car, part of me spoke up. Any one of a cast of characters could have done or said something, but the voice that came commanded the night air with unusual force and conviction. It was as if now was the chance for this suppressed part of me to be heard for once without being immediately told by a stronger part of me to shut up. 'I'm sorry,' I said, 'I have been a complete idiot. I've had a terrible day at work and I shouldn't have been driving like that.' I carried on, pouring out, but as the jug emptied I saw the stark walls of the vessel for the first time. This new voice was clear, and it was one I hadn't heard for a long time. It came from a part of me that knew I was messing up and was desperate to publish that truth. Some-one was at last here to take my confession. It was just a shame it had to be a policeman.

Throughout the questioning that followed, I was fully expecting to be charged. In one sense I wanted it and, if it had come, I would have been handed an opportunity to continue my fight against everything that was conspiring against me. As the lawyer I was then, I would have had something to continue to battle with. Fighting was some-thing I was good at.

After our initial interview the police officer went to check with his colleague in the police car behind. When he came back I realised they'd been checking the ownership of the vehicle, presumably to make sure that I was not simply joyriding in someone else's wheels. Slowly, my story checked out and my initial self-incriminating words hung in the air still, framing my preparedness to accept whatever they had to say. I was happy with this pause in the proceedings; happy to wait for what came next. In truth, I felt lost. My recognition of my own stupidity was so complete that it left me empty, with nowhere familiar to go.

Slowly, as the policeman started to speak, it dawned on me that much as I was ready for whatever they wanted to throw at me, no hammer blow of consequence was coming. The policeman gave me a good ticking off, but it almost seemed that I was like a child best left to be scolded by its mother. I was told there was no charge and that beyond the need to produce my insurance I was free to go. The effect on me was very different, however. I was anything but free. I'd seen something in myself; a trap that I was in. I knew now that I had to deal with it. I could now, because for the first time, I was starting to see the prison I'd made for myself.

I'll never be sure how much the policeman realised the power of what he did that night, but not charging me had a significantly bigger effect than charging me ever would have done. If I had been held to account as a criminal by the police I would have had something to vent my anger at, which would have allowed me to continue my charade. By not charging me they had not only validated my admission but had also released me to take greater responsibility for my own actions from that point. By their putting trust in me, I went away from the incident still entirely focused on my own stupidity, and I got to reflect on the incident and what I was going to learn from it.

The car situation brought me to my senses in the way that life has a habit of doing. The reality is that these moments happen to us all the time on different scales and in different keys. Incident, injury, anger and upset happen to us all and can all pile up. In turn, we either wake up to these situations or we don't. If we don't hear the message they bring, they tend to repeat, often getting bigger and more significant as they recur. Each event has a message for us that we can either bat away or, when we are ready, turn to face.

I'd got myself into this particular situation because I was suffering from the effects power exercised by others was having on me. Instead of seeing this and dealing with it, I was taking the far easier route. Standing up to the abuse of power or taking a different course was too hard. Instead, I was making myself numb to its effects by taking a series of palliatives. At the same time, I was clinging to the system that fed and clothed me and was choosing to pass a version of the abuse I felt on to others. During the day I had taken a few knocks from my boss and a project that I was working on was starting to get some criticism. I'd been defensive, reacting badly to what felt like an assault from the powers that be. I felt attacked and powerless. I felt robbed and wanted my own power back.

Part of my protection against this assault was to cling more tightly to the power I did have, in this case over my car. Part of the deal of the career I was in was that I was paid well to deal with the demands and knocks. It was easier to deal with the pain if the rewards were highly visible and shiny, fitting nicely into my ideal. I now had the sports car I had always wanted as a small boy. My car was so much more than a car – it was a reflection of power, and a reward I could carry myself around in.

In my hands, it was also a tool of power and abuse. The more I was bullied at work the more I could mirror that bullying on the road. In this frame of mind, it became easy to overlook the effects of my actions on others. I didn't see the annoyed pedestrian at the crossing; I didn't notice the mother with a baby out for a bit of air that I blasted past; and I didn't see the countless small disturbances in the human, animal and natural world that I caused. I was lucky nothing worse than being stopped by the police had happened. I was on track to hurt something or someone else. It was one thing for bad to be done to me, but did that really give me an excuse to behave badly to others? I was trapped in a system and couldn't see it. Worse, I could be hypocritical about it. 'Pity me,' I cried, whilst doing absolutely nothing about my own behaviour.

At this point in my life, I now realise most of what I did was framed by the amber, fight part of the traffic light system. This lens was how I saw everything. It was easy for me to see myself in the position of victim to a greater or lesser, more subtle, extent. As such I was often defensive. Cornered, I'd fight, seeing competition as my way forward. If the odds became too high, I might flee, perhaps even slamming the door behind me in anger. I was running away from the things I feared, such as facing up to my dissatisfaction with my work and some of the situations I found myself in. Fear had come to play a dominant role in my life, as both a motivating factor and a constant sparring partner. I'd become used to this way of being; of everything being a battle. A lot of the time I did things because I feared the consequences of not doing them. I did my job because I feared losing it. In turn, I tended to use force and a dose of fear to get what I wanted from others. I saw how easily I could turn into the self-same bully that I loathed. I saw the particular trap I was in, but over time I also saw that

I'd fallen into a way of behaving that was a much more widespread problem.

The book *The Ragged-Trousered Philanthropists* is widely regarded as one of the great classics of working-class literature. It was published in 1914 after the author Robert Noonan's death from tuberculosis three years before. The book explores not only the world of work and its fears (which is in many ways surprisingly unchanged from 1914) but also the socialist solutions that we might embrace and the systemic barriers to them. In his novel, Noonan, who took the pen name of 'Robert Tressell' for the writing of the book but was a house painter by trade, tells the story of a selection of workers who, whilst they suffer to survive and support families, throw themselves into back-breaking work decorating houses in a fictional south coast town in England in the desperately depressed pre-First World War economy. While doing this they all continue to believe that a better life is not for the likes of them. One of the things that Noonan points out is that it is not the individual people themselves who are the root cause of the poverty.

Consistently, all the 'hands', the painters and various trades working on the house, curse Crass, the foreman. These poor souls would, it is pointed out, happily swap roles with their direct boss. However, Noonan notes that if they did swap with him, the truth is that they would have been compelled to act in the same way or lose that self-same job. Likewise, all revile Crass's boss, Hunter, the manager of the firm, but once again realise that given his role they would have ended up driving the workers just as Hunter and Crass did in turn. This goes all the way up to the top, to Rushton, the owner of the enterprise. Even if they had the opportunity to supplant Rushton, who they all ultimately hate and blame, they would end up running the business for maximum profit to avoid ruin. And so it goes on. The danger of having someone to blame is that we don't see the bigger picture, of which we are an intrinsic part.

What we tend to do when we see something we don't like is to focus on the obvious perpetrator. What we miss is that the person we focus on is part of a system. There is a reason why they behave like they do and a reason why they continue to follow the pattern of behaviour that they have adopted. It's like the seaside puppet show of 'Punch and Judy'. If we mostly see the character of Punch we miss what is really going on. In focusing on the villain, we miss that the blow not only has to be struck, it also has to land. Without Judy, there would be no Punch, nor would there be a baby to provide the next generation. It is 'Punch and Judy' that is the show, not 'Punch' alone. Wherever Punch appears, he has his victims lining up. It's important to see that there is something going on here which goes far beyond the characters themselves. Without all the characters, including people who watch, support and benefit from the structure as a whole, it simply wouldn't continue.

Abuses get repeated because the thing that is consistent is the system. Even if we find ourselves to be victims our response is generally not to question the system. Instead it is to change our own status within it. Either we stay as victims, or we copy the strategy that has been practiced upon us by seeking to ascend to a more dominant role ourselves. It is far easier to copy what we see than to change. Our method of responding to threat thus becomes a cycle of copying in which the one thing that never changes is the system itself. The greatest damage that each bully does is not so much the bullying itself as the new bullies that it quietly breeds in turn.

At some point, we humans have to question why we do this.


Our brains have had roughly the size and make-up they do now for some considerable time, estimated to be around 100,000 years. If we travelled back in time to this period in our evolution we'd notice many other things that were very different. First off might be our size. As a measure, 'Lucy', the set of bone fossils of an early walking hominid that was found in 1974, was only 1.1m (3ft 7in) tall. More importantly, we would find that our ancestors were not living at the top of the food chain, as we are now, but rather were still being hunted by large animals, mainly the big cats: tigers, lions, jaguars and leopards. We were, in the early times of walking on two legs, an easy target. We all instinctively know this, because we still feel the shudder of our deep visceral fear at the roar of a lion.

This theory is supported by research done by palaeontologist C.K. Brain, who measured puncture marks in the skulls of the remains of our ancestors found in caves in Southern Africa, which he found to match the distance between the longer teeth of the leopard. What Brain proved was that at this time we were prey rather than predator. This would have been particularly true for weaker members of a group or those who were solitary, who could be more easily caught on the open savannah and dragged back into the big cat's cave to be eaten. This was the environment in which our neural wiring got formed; one in which we expected to be hunted and eaten. In this world, we were all potential victims, and fear was a constant companion.

What we, as a race, have managed to do so well is to create the conditions by which we have been able to master the animals that once hunted us to become the top predator. Like the bullied victim who chooses the easy option to become the bully, what we have done is simply take the place of the big cat. What we haven't done is to change the prey-based system itself. Meanwhile, the beasts that we once feared are now locked up in zoos or are more controlled in the wild so they are no longer the systemic threat that they once were.

I call this strategy of predation our 'Monkey'. We are no longer monkeys, but by continuing to follow this strategy we continue to be beholden to something we adopted from the animal world. The original predator, who we mimic, was just being a lion. The apes and monkeys felt fear and they were right to do so. As an animal, fear is a helpful thing to feel. We are more than just animals, though. Consciousness gave us the ability to choose our own strategies. Given this capacity it is a fair choice to no longer want to be a lion's lunch. But in adopting Monkey's strategy into our own psychology as humans, the problem today is that man has let it affect his consciousness. Crucially, Monkey is still scared. This is ironic, because the lion that scared our Monkey in the first place was never afraid.

What Monkey has done for us so far and so well is to simply copy the tigers and lions that we once feared. This is perhaps why these predatory animals appear so often as symbols of power on our buildings, structures and vehicles. The lion, the jaguar and the great predatory eagle represent power. The system of predation itself, of victim and villain, remains deeply within us, held in place by the fear Monkey has of the original predator and any replacement predator Monkey can find. This is why we so easily cast ourselves as the victims and are so easily drawn to stories of victimisation. Monkey's belief is that there is always a hierarchy. We admire those 'above' us as we are wary of those 'below' us. Monkey's strategy, then, is to accept and to ascend that hierarchy. It is this belief and this compulsive strategy that now make it so difficult to allow power to be distributed more equally to all.

As long as we continue to carry it forward, the Monkey strategy locks fear into the system. If our solution to the fear we experience is to become predators ourselves, then we haven't yet addressed the real issue. If our route to safety sits in our ascent of the hierarchy, then we sit in that hierarchy still carrying fear. It may feel like the house, the car or the role protects us, but psychologically, where it really matters, this armour is never quite enough. Behind the shield, we remain in fear; afraid to be naked. Like the bully, we are still a victim whether we sit atop the hierarchy or elsewhere in it. It actually doesn't matter where we are; we will either inflict fear on ourselves or allow others to do it for us. The truth is that even the bully who we feel sits on top feels like a victim. The feeling never goes away. That is because it is the fear we continue to carry with us, like an addiction. But like any addiction, it is not a requirement, it is optional.

As well as not being afraid, our original predator also had no choice. It had no apple offered to it in the Garden of Eden. We are different in that we have consciousness; our gift of imagination, which allows us to see options and to choose. That same gift to imagine, which separates us from animals, is what makes us a victim of our fears. Now it is time to understand that fear rather than be consumed by it. Because we have the ability to choose, we have the ability to change all of our strategies, including this one. This is where the tipping point lies. Do we really want to stop at this stage in our evolution if we are going to continue to be afraid? This is power based on fear. If we stick with Monkey's strategy, we remain vulnerable, even if we think we have triumphed. This is where I was when I was speeding; trapped.

What we have done has been highly successful. We've adopted a strategy from our predator and used it to get ourselves to the top of the pile. What we don't seem to have ever done is stop and think about our human objectives or strategy. This is something that nobody tends to do until there is a clear and obvious problem with the original strategy. I didn't stop until I was stopped by the police. In the meantime, we race ever onwards with the solution to the original problem but haven't stopped to ask ourselves why we are doing *this,* and more particularly, this *now.* What we haven't done yet is to change the system of predation itself. We are living in a very different world but Monkey still easily dominates our collective behaviour. Our internal default wiring is still very much aligned to the system that we grew up in, for the most part as victims of that system.

Reflecting back on the time I was stopped by the police, what I find most surprising now was that I felt so put upon when I was actually so privileged. I started my career as a lawyer and was fortunate, early in my working life, to be given a lot of responsibility. For many years I was a negotiator of deals for big corporates. When I first started at it I was essentially still a young lawyer. I was rubbish at it. I was far too aggressive and conceited. One of the many mistakes I made, in what was essentially an 'Alpha male' style of getting what I wanted, was to think I had power to dominate others, when that simply wasn't the case. Something in my own strategies and training told me I could. When I banged the table and got angry, I thought I was doing that as a dominant power player. That was partly true. I was a player – but I was the victim rather than the villain, part of a system. The loud complaining marked me out as someone who had lost their power and had no options left other than to make a noise. Even in the jungle it is the quiet lion that has the power; noise speaks of something else. Incessant noise is a signal that things are not well.

The incident that evening in my car brought home to me how easily I could cast myself in the role of victim. It didn't matter what power I achieved, because I retained the habit of putting myself back in that role. I was lucky to have been caught like I was. Just like I started to wake up that night, we all have an opportunity. The policeman jolted me back into consciousness, but by offering a hand of trust as a friend rather than the adversary I expected, he reset my framing of the situation into the safe friendly zone, where I was able to engage fully with what was really going on. The fighting ended and power shifted. Instead of externalising the problem, I took responsibility for myself. I moved from amber to green. The same is true of Monkey. For Monkey to persist in becoming his own predator would be to come up short in the long game. We have the opportunity to evolve beyond simply copying everyone else's strategy of preying on someone even less fortunate. To truly move ahead of the predator, we have to move beyond stealing another's approach as a temporary measure. We have to create a new strategy of our own.

This is, however, starting to move into an argument to do the right thing again and potentially another break in my original promise. It is also a clue that we haven't got to the bottom of the problem yet. Monkey is only part of the issue. We are dealing with a scared and highly determined Monkey. He is not going to give up easily. He has also cleverly found a co-conspirator who has done a lot of work to create a narrative that supports him. It is this narrative and the way this consolidates Monkey's position that we need to look at next.

What irritates you?

# 4. Scared Stories

In 2013, I finally made a big jump. I didn't launch myself out of an aeroplane or jump off a high building, but nevertheless as I stepped out of the familiar structure I knew, into empty space, the act of letting go felt just like stepping into free fall. For all my reservations, I'd now worked for big organisations in paid employment for over 20 years. The jump came after a conversation with my boss at the time. The final thing I did before I made the jump was to phone my wife to tell her that I was going to resign from my job without having another 'job' to go to. To this day I am surprised just how supportive she was, and within minutes I was writing my resignation letter.

The actions I was taking felt surreal but also had an inevitable, flowing quality to them. It was almost as if I was in a movie, following an unseen script that I didn't quite understand. Some, as yet unvoiced, subterranean part of me felt relieved, entirely comfortable with the way the story was unfolding, as the more familiar rest of me screamed, 'What the hell are you doing!'

I had avoided taking this step for years. I had told myself that the risks of leaving a secure, well-paid job were too great. Rationally I was right. I was the commercial director of a decent-sized business. Every time I looked at how much I'd need to earn to replace my income, to support my family, I concluded that earning that sort of money for myself would be an insurmountable task. For years I'd flirted with the idea of leaving, but the fear of making the jump, the sheer terror of the step into the void, had always stopped me, and I continued to tease at the edge.

But once I did jump, it didn't feel like a jump at all. I realised that the story I had built was a myth, and the metaphor I'd chosen was not just inadequate, it was plain wrong. Now I was here, I saw that it was entirely different from everything I'd ever imaged it to be. I had a sense of wonder as I found out that nothing I'd imagined before was of any practical use. I saw the gap between imagination and reality and all I felt was relief and calm. The ground had not disappeared from beneath me after all. The earth that I was walking on now was still there; just the same as it had been before.

Although I'd quietly been preparing to take a step out for years, the moment itself came as a surprise. My boss and I disagreed on the way forward. I'd had a series of warning signs, some of which I'd noticed and some of which I'd chosen not to notice. They resulted from the strategy I was pursuing with my team. It was based on giving them more responsibility and control and helping them to grow. This approach was working well and they were starting to step up their game. I'd been recruited to do this, having done exactly the same in a previous job.

My problem was that my boss no longer agreed with my approach. It had become clear that both our principles and our models of operation differed. In one example, he'd told me to fire a member of my team and I'd refused to do so. We were starting to differ on more than one issue like this, and that difference was crystallising. What I'd conveniently forgotten was that in the hierarchical world I was in, he was the boss, and if he wanted to control things, ultimately he could. Finally, the matter came to a head in a meeting that I left with no illusion remaining as to what our differences were.

I decided to go, and the day I resigned, I took the plunge into a new world that miraculously opened up for me. In the years that have passed, I have never once looked back. A year later I asked myself how I felt about what I was doing compared to the day after I had resigned. The answer was 'more committed'. The following year I asked myself the same question compared to the previous year, and the answer was 'more committed'. Now I ask myself this question every year and notice I get the same answer. I also notice why I get the same answer and how my vision of who I am and what I am doing has refined itself. In this exercise of looking back and comparing my experience now to my fears then, it's clear that all of the fears that I had before I made the jump were incorrect. My fear was a fiction, dreamt up by my overprotective mind.

As I've looked at fear through my own eyes, and increasingly those of others, I see that this is a big chunk of the problem. The Lion may not have been afraid, but we are, and it is our mind that makes us so. We are like a child sleeping alone in a house, who hears something downstairs. The sound of the wind or a creak as the house moves becomes something else in our imagination. Soon we can hear a dangerous burglar creeping around downstairs, about to get us. It doesn't take long for our fertile imagination to build a rich tapestry of possibility based on that one sound. Even as adults, our fears work on the same basis. It is the story we make up that scares us, not what is actually happening. Seldom do we have real evidence for the narrative we have led ourselves to believe. The stories our overthinking mind makes up are what truly scare us. If we were honest, we'd admit there is a flaw in our mind. The problem is that we need to remember who it is that we are trying to convince that this is so. It is our mind itself. It's like trying to tell someone who's absolutely convinced they're right that they are in fact wrong; it tends not to go down well. What's more, we are generally on our own, acting as participant, judge and jury, as well as our own counsel, as we do it.

These stories make us in at least two different ways. In any moment, we tend to be both living a narrative and creating one from the new situations we find ourselves in. In this chapter, we are going to look primarily at the narratives we have created already which tend, if we are not aware of it, to unwittingly control our behaviour and thus our lives. These narratives do this because they affect our sense of identity. We become our own reaction to fear. To illustrate this, I'm going to share my own narrative. The process of understanding stories like this is a bit like an archaeological dig, except that the work is never fully complete. It might reach a stage where it feels done, but my experience is that there is always more to be uncovered. Just like a dig, every site and piece of archaeology is different, but once you get the idea there are patterns you will get familiar with and some tools you might like to try for yourself.

In sidestepping my own narrative, one of the things I have learned to do is to take on challenges that I have no idea how I will deliver. In order to do this, I generate and talk about possibility in the direction I want to go even if I haven't yet worked out the details. This can feel terrifying, however. When I was first asked to lead a leadership workshop in the early days of being self-employed I was overcome by a wave of terror that threatened to engulf my response. All my feelings of being an unworthy imposter lined up, circled round me, and deafened me with their reasons for why I had no right to do this. Instead of letting these feelings limit me, I learned to master a committed voice that simply said 'sure' as if I did these things all the time. The future me had spoken even if the present me was recoiling in hidden, inner panic.

In this conflict, what I can see is that parts of me live in the world of possibility whilst other parts of me live in a world of certainty. The danger is that the default setting that defines me, if I let it, will be that of certainty and structure, the known and the safe. I know I can be pretty good in the world I've already mastered, so it's a highly attractive and easy route to getting a lot of what I think I want. It is easy to just keep doing what I already do well. The problem with this world is that it is my past, so anything I build using it, however improved, can only ever be a version of my past. By following the certain route all I am doing is creating my future in the self-limiting image of what I already know. That might be a good thing if I'm happy to be a master of an unchanging traditional craft, but not if I want to explore my potential.

What I found was that the feeling of stepping into thin air, of allowing myself to be in what could feel like free fall, was essential for me to create a future that was different. Ironically, it is only by being uncomfortable that we become more comfortable. We grow our comfort zone by stepping into discomfort and, over time, claiming it. There is no growth for me in the safe, structured world because all it wants me to do is to stay the same, doing the same things. If we stay in comfort, comfort doesn't even stay the same; it shrinks. To avoid a shrinking island, we have to learn to put at least one foot into the world of the uncomfortable, even if we keep the other in comfort. If we're growing, the territory around us is unfamiliar and throws up genuine obstacles that we haven't learned to work through before. It is in this messy working through that all the breakthroughs in growth happen. Unfortunately, truly courageous leadership doesn't feel like a nicely structured and level parade ground. It feels more like a sticky swamp.

One of the methods I have identified that allows me to take on a challenge more easily is to simply put it in the diary. It is a commitment, but it is in the future. My reasoning is that by the time it arrives I will have worked out how to do it and how to face it. Time and time again, this approach has proved to be something that works. Through this slightly deferred commitment to a scary future, I've started to normalise and get confident with the feelings I get as the big scary thing approaches. Even if I haven't done the thing before, I've felt this way before and I know that last time I got through it. And when the thing does arrive, I'm increasingly learning that either I'll be ready, or that I have the confidence that I'll find a way to face the challenge in the moment. So far, this strategy has paid off, however much my mind tells me that it won't.

What I've also noticed is that I am not always as committed to these things happening as the diary date indicates. I notice this perhaps when I haven't booked travel arrangements or a hotel. Part of this lack of commitment is chosen – I don't want to plan what I'm going to do months in advance – but part of it indicates that I haven't fully committed. I've learned to be comfortable with this feeling and that booking the flights, the train tickets or the hotel is part of the journey that starts to make my commitment real. It also provides me with a feedback loop. What is going on here, and why is my commitment being challenged?

I have learned over time to listen to how I feel about the challenges I face and, in particular, how I react to them. It's hardly surprising that I'd react differently to some than others, but what is a surprise is that the uncomfortable build-ups are not necessarily linked to the obvious big events. One of these came on a train idling gently through the countryside from Cambridge to Norwich late one afternoon. I was on the way to an engagement the following day. It was the first time I'd delivered an all-day training session based on my work for a corporate client. I'd decided to do the two-hour-plus journey the day before and stay overnight. I was going to Norwich and wanted to have a wander around the city centre whilst things were still open and before it got dark.

Now, as I sat on the train, heading though the flat misty fenland, I noticed that I was substantially more nervous than I would expect. I didn't understand this, as I wasn't facing hundreds of people or speaking without notes. For once, I had handouts and a presentation to put up on the screen to speak to. Fortunately, the early arrival and the slow train had an unexpected benefit, as I had the time to ask myself why I was feeling so nervous. I'd noticed the sense of unease creeping up on me for the last few days and had filed it away for the future rather than choosing to meet it head on. As I sat there, with the train taking care of the journey, I relaxed and faced the feeling, asking myself, 'Why this and why now?'

Sitting at a table on the train, I got out my notebook and wrote at the top of the page 'Why am I uncomfortable?' I then sat with the odd feeling that I had and accepted it. Immediately, it had more texture. As I accepted it, it ceased to be just a surface feeling and instead opened up and spoke to me. I could distinctly feel that parts of me that anchored themselves firmly in the world of safety and certainty were feeling under threat. Down the left-hand side of the page I captured these individual feelings.

Then, down what I still had of the right-hand side of the page, I squeezed into the remaining margin what I felt my challenge was. All of this poured out in a matter of a few minutes. When I'd done it, I sat back and looked at it. In the short time that had passed my entire mood had changed. All my nerves had gone and the weight that had been building up on me all week had suddenly lifted.

---

### Why am I uncomfortable?

| | |
|---|---|
| My expert smarty pants is going to be tested | Good. He's ready. Curtail him though – it's about them, not you! |
| My control hates the newness, the uncertainty | Yes, but the fun lies in the new and the unknown and you know that! |
| My need to be right is bound to be challenged | Yes! It damn well needs to be. How about allowing others to be right occasionally? |

---

What most surprised me was that by giving up control in one sense I was more in control in another. Ironically, by facing up to a character that was always about getting more control, I now had more control over who I was. This false god of control was stopping me from moving into the new space where I wanted to be. My way through was to see the character and to start to deal with the grip that it had over my behaviour. In doing this I was making a breakthrough. I had previously been blind to the way the character affected my behaviour.

Now I could not only see it, I could also choose to stop it from taking control away from me in a live situation.

I could also see how it wasn't just one character that affected me. There were multiple characters, and they could easily show up in a group. If they were on the train they would be sitting around a table arguing and raising merry hell. Although they were slightly different in their tastes something would bring them together so that they'd end up dragging round sets of supermarket beer cans in six-pack rings. They'd be stoked up by each other like a noisy group on the way to a football match, all challenging one another, upping the ante. The power of the group helped each of its members to hold and then express a more extreme view. Together, they were even more dangerous.

At one point, I drew each character out and identified a human form for each by thinking of someone who, for me, represented their behaviour. I had a partly Formula 1 theme in that David Coulthard was my expert, Bernie Ecclestone was my control and 1970s TV cook Fanny Cradock, for some curious but mostly unknown reason, was my need to be right. This gave me a shock when I realised that all the real people I choose for my characters were people I disliked without understanding why. This was its own breakthrough, as I then realised that I disliked these characters for no reason other than I saw my own behaviour in them. I was escaping from my own challenge by transferring it to someone else. I could see that this strategy stopped me from seeing who these people and others like them really were. This was something beautifully brought home to me when I unexpectedly met David Coulthard in the children's section of a bookshop in Barcelona Airport and immediately liked him. I realised he was totally different in reality from how I'd seen him. It wasn't him I disliked at all – it was something in me.

In playing with these characters I also realised that they could come together in one character. I got to this by dwelling on a series of possible candidates and checking out how well they worked for me. After a few false starts I settled on a continuance of the racing theme as I tested a retired racing driver who lived in the middle of an old abandoned circuit. He was perfect. In the racing driver, I saw the dragging force of this character on me as he struggled to get out in the world and do anything. Why should he, when he had the option of resting securely on what he thought were his laurels? Night by night he ran circuits in the safety of his own world, convinced he could beat anyone whilst the world moved on, oblivious to him. That picture, more than anything, helped me to break the grip this character and his behaviours had over me. There was no way I wanted to let this stuck old has-been run things.

We tend to think of growth as a slow, linear thing, but my experiences made me question this. I found I'd get to a point and then feel stuck. My choice then was how I went forward from there. The solution to this felt more like a series of breakthroughs not unlike the moulting stages that crustaceans such as lobsters and crabs go through as they shed one shell in order to form another. As we change and grow, the old shell just gets tighter and tighter. The frustration of our old structure slowly builds up on us. Finally, we come to a point where we know we have to shed the old shell. The strategy that at first protected us now restricts us. What had made me uncomfortable on the train was this partly suppressed conflict between the limiting structure of my old shell and the new form emerging within. My discomfort in the old shell was a sign. It was also something to be welcomed and understood rather than something to be avoided, numbed or medically treated, as I might have sought to do in the past.

The shellfish model worked because it was only by stepping into my discomfort and understanding it that I had managed to grow through this stage. My discomfort went as soon as I made my realisation, even though I hadn't yet worked out how I was going to fix it. Understanding the problem mattered more than having a fully thought-out solution to it. I felt that it was only by experimenting that I'd find a new way forward anyway. I had to have confidence that I'd work that out in practice and perhaps just the awareness was all I needed to change my behaviour. Just like the lobster, I was free to grow again, even if I might have to be careful for a while as I tried out my softer, more vulnerable shell.

If the natural course of my life was like a river in flow, I was starting to see that these characters had ended up layered over one another, blocking the flow. They were operating like a thick-matted dam that simply acquired more clutter as the river brought more building material downstream. I was asking for a life that was in flow, but I was constantly held back by blockages. I couldn't easily see exactly what was blocking the flow, but I could feel that something was in the way.

I then realised that my need for control and to be right, the things that formed the structure I now felt so constrained by, hadn't just come from nowhere. Part of me was at work constructing this. As I started to notice the structures I was holding onto, I found a Beaver, busy at work, building a narrative structure out of everything. The more scared I was, the more the narrative built up. Every time I felt I had to defend myself against what my Monkey saw as an attack, Beaver worked with the Monkey, building a story around my actions to defend me. My ego owned the dam and was building a safe structure in the middle of the stream of my life.

As I watched I saw what happened when the river threatened to flood, or when the structure was overwhelmed momentarily, or when a part of the dam was washed away. The Beaver was constantly at work, rebuilding the structure. However much I was concerned about getting the flow back and pushing for it, I also had a character that saw fixing the dam as his job. Busy Beaver had taken material from my life and had built an impressive, safe home out of it. Like any large built structure, it required constant maintenance, but the Beaver was happy to do it. He had a job to do and sharp teeth. Woe betide anyone who questioned that.

I was only seeing these characters with me on the train because I'd started investigating how I behaved in response to stressful events from a different perspective. What I'd started to do was to look at the timeline of my early life and to think about big moments I still remembered, particularly those where I'd felt threatened. As I looked at these events I started to see connections between them. I then started to build a hypothesis of how I'd built up a behaviour or a belief in reaction to what happened. This wasn't easy, as I'd reached a point where my reactive strategy was now so much a part of who I was that I couldn't see it any more. My way of behaving generally operated in my 'blind spot', a place that was annoyingly out of my sight.

This also meant that when I or anyone else challenged these behaviours my first reaction was usually to deny that I had a problem. Now what I was doing was testing them, challenging myself to see something that, however visible it might be to others, conspired to remain hidden from me.

What this 'Beaver' part of our mind does is to create a narrative that takes these critical instances when we are threatened and builds a defensive strategy out of them. This strategy then becomes so well fixed that we don't notice it any more. It is like a play that is repeated to different audiences night after night. A stage play takes this idea of a fixed narrative and literally plays it out. Shakespeare was a master of this, and in *As You Like It* he takes the idea and gives it back to us, presenting us with the idea that the whole world is a stage on which we are merely players.

Shakespeare's 'All the world's a stage' statement begins a famous monologue that is one of his most frequently quoted passages. In it, the idling philosophical thinker, Jaques, also gives us his idea of the 'seven ages of man'. In these seven ages, there are three crucial ones in our early life before we are propelled into the world of 'soldier' in the fourth age. These are 'infant', 'schoolboy' and 'lover'. If we accept that each age is a rough period of about seven years, we get essentially three periods – infant until about seven, schoolchild broadly seven to 14, and lover in the period 14 to the milestone period of 21. These ages can help to give us a clue to our 'players'.

In the first, infant stage, we are building a core part of who we are in relationship with our closest caregiver. In the schoolchild stage, we are branching out into our first social relationships, usually at school. In the lover stage, we are embarking on closer affectionate and physical relationships and branching out into the ever-wider world. But our narrative doesn't get built by a playwright. It gets built by us, in response to events early on in our lives.

If we look back at the river of our lives we can see that it wasn't always blocked with a dam. The structure of who we are may look solid now, but what we have done is to build the characters that make up the dam in stages. We might remember one event, but the more significant strategies tend to arise from a series of connected experiences. They get stronger as they are repeated over time. This is not a question of what actually happened, but more about how we experienced events and the story we made up in order to make sense of them and to build protection against similar threats going forward. Whilst we are not looking, our Beaver builds an explanatory narrative that prepares us for the future. Soon we can't even tell the difference between what actually happened and the defensive story our beavering ego has created to deal with the perceived threat it contained.

The threat we feel in the situation often comes from someone with good intentions. It might even have been made by someone very close to us whose intentions were entirely loving, but that is not the issue here. It's not the motivation of the loving parent or carer we are questioning but rather the interpretation of the delicate youth. Often the narrative has no logical justification; it doesn't need to. Instead, what we are interested in is how we experienced what happened and how we built our own internal story of how we needed to be in response.

When I looked at my early years I connected strongly to a sense of being left, or perhaps choosing, to fend for myself. I could never get anything right and was always in trouble. I remember being caught by the police and the police reporting me to my parents. The adult world was trying to help me by imposing discipline on a wayward young man, but had the opposite effect as I rebelled more deeply by resisting. By opposing that authority, I became, at the same time, more convinced of my own authority. As a result, I tended to play alone in the woods and read a lot. I felt the joy of self-sufficiency, but the truth was that I was getting cut off. I drew a pig-headed strength from the feeling that *they* were wrong and that *I* was right. I could not see that I was getting trapped in the loner narrative I was building.

It is a more general irony in life that we either tend to adopt something wholeheartedly or we reject it in rebellion, becoming the opposite. If we have a religious parent, for example, we might become similarly devout, or we may flip to the contrary view and become agnostic. This 'adopt or fight' polarity tends to affect most things, including politics, where the middle struggles to survive. It is a consequence of an approach that puts us in one camp or the other, but the irony is completed in the terrible inevitability that we tend to become what we fight the most. What we resist persists, and in a curious *Animal Farm*-style hypocrisy we can end up unwittingly copying the exact behaviour we most oppose. Ultimately, we run the risk of becoming what we set out to fight. Fighting authority had this effect on me, as I sought to build my own.

As I started to think back to my 'second age' of seven to 14, I recalled my response to a period of bullying in the early years of secondary school. It tended to happen as we left the music block, which was detached from the rest of the school. I remembered that I sat next to the door to get out quick. This was a physical thing I did, but my underlying strategy was to be smarter than everyone else, including the teachers, who, in my eyes, did nothing to help. Being clever also worked in practical terms; it eventually got me into a different class from the bully. In this experience, I saw the origins of my 'smart expert' character, which also built on my loner narrative. I started to see how these characterisations could work together or build upon one another.

I could also see how in the 14–21 'lover' stage the theme of control had got stronger as a solution to failures in early relationships that were partly caused by the defensive character I had. As my earliest significant relationship floundered, I reacted brutally to my partner's vulnerability and cut the relationship off in order to achieve the control I sought. As I moved out of my teens and into my early twenties I turned this into a need for career success, which became essential to me as a way to prove myself.

It was this work that enabled me to understand my discomfort on the Norwich train. In this disquiet I could see how I tended to play on the world's stage. I see these behaviours as characters and call them the Power Players. For me the three that captured what I felt on the train were my 'Expert', 'Control' and 'Need to be Right'. At any time, any one of these characters can take over my behaviour and turn me into someone who imposes their view on others. I know deep down that this is unhelpful, but at the same time I am habitually addicted to the behaviour and thus struggle do anything else. We all create our own different Power Players in response to the events in our own lives. In this way, the threats we feel are visited on us by the world get to come and live in us. In turn, we visit them on others, cultivating a climate of fear.

The irony of these characters was that I had created them originally to protect myself, but I now saw that they were dominating me. It was almost as if I had built my own internal army: a series of villains, working on the inside, whose intent was to systematically fight against me ever being a victim again. In this crazy war, my openness to growth was the first casualty. This safety net had a price. The defensive structure was robustly built, but it had me rather than me having it.

As if this wasn't enough, my success was intertwined with what these characters had done for me. By my mid 30s I was successful at being an expert, in control, who was right. What better thing to become than a lawyer? If part of me hadn't had an itch to change, a knowledge that this track wasn't really for me and a desire to broaden my enquiry, I would probably still be there, doing something that wasn't really me at all. For a while I couldn't see past the structure. The dam that Beaver had built completely hid from my view who I really was.

I also noticed that my busy Beaver takes no rest and likes to go out and fell trees and flood plains far beyond the dam itself. His main additional hobby is to create narratives about specific people and situations. I left my job because I disagreed with my boss, but I also now saw that I'd created a story about who he was and the faults he had. As I built the narrative in my head I also watched myself seek to triangulate that story with others as I sought support for the things I felt about him. As I found additional evidence, the story reinforced itself. As he became bad, I became better. This is what the Beaver narrative does. After a while, the story was as addictive and self-satisfying as a powerful drug.

Essentially what we do here is to build on the difference between our enhanced knowledge of our own situation and our lack of knowledge of the other's situation. This effect itself is known as the fundamental attribution error. What this does is to recognise that we tend to attribute our own bad behaviour to rational, legitimate reasons but see the similar actions of others as foolishness at best. Thus, if I run a red light, I know that I did it for a good reason: I had no opportunity to stop. However, if I see someone else doing exactly the same, they are a reckless danger to humanity, out to kill someone. Our explanations for the internal and the external differ based on the widely different levels of understanding we have of each.

The problem with this emerging narrative is that it builds justification for staying exactly as we are, fixed and positional. Any discomfort we might feel is explained away. If I can make up a reason for the other being wrong, then I am right to be as I am. This growing story in turn makes it more difficult for me to see my faults and to contemplate any question of change myself. I call this narrative our 'Standing Story'.

We have Standing Stories about everything. We can see ourselves building them and relying on them whenever our views about anything become fixed. In them we make ourselves bigger and the other person smaller. It is a back-door method of imposing on others to make us feel better about ourselves. As soon as we have a Standing Story we have stopped listening to that person or appreciating them for what they are. Instead we are builders, looking for evidence to support our story. We can even adopt a story from others in our tribe. You may have your own reasons for disliking your neighbour Betty, but it's easy for me, because you don't like Betty, to not like her either. Our lazy copying Monkey likes to outsource judgement whenever it can. The human world sits on a rich tapestry of Standing Stories.

Standing Stories are easy to spot. As soon as we start to have a fixed view about anyone or anything, it is worth considering whether we can really see the situation or the other person as they really are. We get to feel better about ourselves, but in that there is a cost; our view about the situation is locked. If they changed, would we notice? The position we have taken benefits our ego but it also adds fodder to the great blocked-up dam in our river that our Beaver is happy to keep building.

Together all these elements of narrative build up and hold us in a certain place. That place will be different for each of us, as will the force that holds us there. The danger with this narrative is that we can become deeply committed to it without ever really seeing what it does to us. Then, when we want to grow and to change, it blocks us. We carry the baggage of our stories around with us blindly. If I am unwittingly controlled by my expert narrative, for example, I'll end up interrupting someone to put them right. As my expert speaks up, perhaps aiming at control, it will crowd out what might otherwise have happened. These deeply held but mostly unacknowledged commitments are what stop us from changing as they take over the available space from the things we'd really like to do but keep failing at. They are built on fear and they create a climate of fear around them, not just for us but also for our own victims in turn.

In the end, my career jump was a long overdue step. I had thought that a career change was all about what I did. I began to see instead that it was as much, if not more, about who I was. I didn't just get to reinvent my work. I got to rediscover and grow myself.

As I looked back on the events that had led to my leaving, I saw that even the disagreements I'd had with my ex-boss in the last months revolved around how my Power Players had clashed with his. We were both people who sought to be right and to take control; experts in our own ways. These things lay at the heart of the achievements that solidified who we were. These same things that had helped us also led to the clash. I saw that in ceding control to these characters I had allowed myself to become more of a defensive victim than I needed to be. The Standing Stories I created about him added to the mess, as I was unable to see my boss as he really was. Instead I was lost in the fog of my own stories about him.

We all have challenges like this to deal with, and life isn't going to stop throwing threats at us tomorrow. Our question is more about how we see them and whether our response is appropriate. It is a bit like having a healthy immune system. One of the things the immune system does when it kicks in is to take over. It might raise our temperature and make us want to rest, but it does this for a reason. It helps us to focus our resources to deal with the infection. Much as this might help us deal with a virus every so often, an overactive immune system that is always kicking in or one that holds us in that reactive state permanently would hold us in a state of defence when we no longer need to be so. That state of continual defence is both tiring and limiting. What is more, we know now that this does happen. In the immune system, we recognise this overactive or dysfunctional state as 'autoimmunity'.

Monkey and Beaver together are a great team, but the work they do is can be like having an overactive immune system. The list of recognised autoimmune diseases, such as multiple sclerosis, type 1 diabetes and rheumatoid arthritis, has grown to at least 80 today from the first recognised condition in the early 1900s and the list continues to grow. As time goes on, we are learning more about what causes these diseases and the potential links between them. In the future, we may even see a connection between the physical and the psychological immune system. In the meantime, I believe fear thrives in the mind just as illness does in the body, and that we should be searching for answers to it in a similar way.

Monkey and Beaver are an accomplished act. Monkey is a vitriolic combatant with an inflated sense of ego who is smart enough to employ Beaver as his busy subaltern to write a compelling narrative. Just like any committed leader with an efficient PR person at their side, this team can control history if we let them.

It doesn't end here though. Just as Monkey doesn't work alone, Monkey and Beaver don't either. The pair get to operate within an overarching system of power that goes much wider. This system is our final port of call on the 'what stops us' part of the equation. Now we are going to meet this overall framework of power in which fear lives. In the next chapter, we will dig down to understand Imposed Power and how we allow fear to feed itself.

What behavioural patterns do you have?

# 5. Imposed Power

Sue is a regular at a sailing club where I spend at least a week every year teaching kids how to sail. Sue has the job of organising the ramp on which the children launch their boats. The ramp starts in a narrow gateway which then immediately crosses a busy sea-wall footpath. This is followed by a sharp bend and a road-width of concrete down into the muddy water brought in by the incoming tide. The boats are of different shapes, and many of them are barely held together with patched wooden repairs and bits of string. For a brief period when they launch and later when they come back we have approaching a hundred boats and even more children all moving around in a relatively small space. Sue is the strong personality who organises this rather busy system, a system that is easily prone to falling into chaos.

What Sue does is to rigorously police a structure that everyone respects and which works. In the launching phase, she only allows trailers through the gate and onto the ramp in their teaching groups of some six to twelve boats at a time. She is also ruthless about these groups having to be ready, with their sails up. If a group is not ready she may let another group that is ready go ahead. Because this is not really about boats at all but about the trailers they sit on, she also has a one-way system, where boats go down one side of the ramp, with the empty trailers coming back up the other side. The trailers are then stored by groups with coloured tags and clearly labelled sail numbers so that they can be quickly recovered when the group decides to come back in.

All this is a bit much to take in at once, but Sue has a system and a group of volunteers who also know the system, who help to run things. Like the cogs in a complex clock movement, the people at the top of the ramp interlink with those in the middle who, in turn, work with those at the bottom. A spare volunteer soon finds a gap that needs them. Somehow there is always someone to take each trailer off each child as their boat goes in the water. This allows each child or pair of children to get in their boats quickly. All in all, it is a well-oiled machine that has evolved over a number of years and continues to be refined.

Talking to a variety of children over the years, I have noticed that Sue affects each of them differently. Many are simply afraid of her and the possibility of being called out. The system works partly because of the compliance that fear breeds in them. For other kids, it is just a structure that exists which they mostly have to comply with and will be told if they don't. Some kids even test Sue out, to see where the boundaries are. What I most noticed, though, was my own reaction to it as an adult instructor, as someone who perhaps should know better. My problem, if I am honest, is that I've never really liked structure. I am always designing my way round it at best and, frankly, rebelling against it at worst. I was surprised, then, that this wasn't the way I reacted here. In my wider life, I'd started to think that I just couldn't accept the rigidity of structures and systems but now, here, Sue's set-up helped me to realise that this wasn't the case. I would be the first to complain if there was no Sue. Here, with the boats, there would be carnage. This would also be true in many other places. Without structure, cars would crash into each other on the roads and things would start to break down all over the area, county and country. It wasn't having a system or process that bothered me. I realised that it was something else altogether.

What I objected to was being imposed upon. I routinely moved away from, designed my way round and rejected the imposition of power by one person over another. What I really disliked was being forced to do something I didn't want to do. This, ultimately, is the behaviour that Monkey's strategy is responsible for. It is a system of power that is so sunk into the framework surrounding everything that we do, it has become quite difficult to see. Just like the bus that surrounded the dinosaur, it is there, but we tend not to notice it. I call this framework 'Imposed Power' because it acts upon us as an imposition. Imposed Power builds on the behaviour of Monkey's predator. It is built on the belief that power is something external to us and something that we expect to act upon us. It could be in the form of a gentle nudge (if we don't do this, that'll happen) or a more solid push (the screams of the sergeant-major). It is a form of power that we have largely grown up to expect; the ability to require someone to do something ultimately by force or coercion if necessary. It can still feel like our original predator. In shape, it can be sharp, aggressive and mechanical. It pushes down on us, and in its presence we tend to feel smaller. Like any predator, it sees our weaknesses. In the presence of Imposed Power, we are stopped from speaking the truth we want to speak. Our true feelings make us feel vulnerable to attack, so we hide them. In its presence we are fearful, and we are fearful for a reason. Fear thrives in this environment, like a rat in a sewer.

Sue's approach is entirely different. When I watched Sue at work I realised that even though sometimes it might seem like a form of Imposed Power, it had none of Monkey's bite. There was no monster here but rather an intent to help everyone. When I spoke to Sue about it she told me that although this was her holiday, her main occupation was her job as a headteacher in a school for children with special needs. As she spoke to me about her beliefs and how she deeply cared for every one of the children in her school individually, I understood what drove her. I also saw why she is the leader she is. She can't help but to reach out and to help. Sue has no inbuilt desire for power, she just does what she needs to do to enable others. The irony is that this leads her into leadership roles, and even though her team and the system could now operate without her, Sue is in demand and loved for what she does. She is even known by many simply, and somewhat fondly, as 'Ramp Sue'. Most importantly Sue is an innovator. She is open to any ideas that might improve the system. Ultimately, she knows it is not so much her system but everyone's. I felt no imposition because none was intended.

In the world at large, Imposed Power persists and works because we fear the consequences of failing to heed it. It and the fear it engenders is thus a primary tool of control, used by anyone who wants to grab it for themselves. In turn, when we choose to pick it up and use it ourselves, we tend to impose upon others. It is the framework that we also see in the amber, fight/flight zone of the traffic light. Here we tend to see things through the lens of Imposed Power. Fundamentally, this is about a prey-based belief system that underpins much of our thinking and thus our behaviour. It's a belief that winning and having control is what is important. It cares much less about the consequences. In this game, if I win, it is at your expense. The problem is that whilst the battle rages, we are both in fear of the outcome. Ultimately, if we don't get what we want, we can resort to fighting for it. This war-like understanding of how power is exercised tends to sit in the framework that surrounds our thinking about how anything challenging gets done. As way of being that filters the lens of how things are done, it's a subtle thing that we are generally blind to. This approach may work for pair of gladiators or to help win a tennis match, but what we are in danger of doing is extending it to everything we do in our wider lives. It is a strategy, as opposed to a necessity. When I was caught speeding, I had allowed my life to be full of Imposed Power. I didn't have to, but I had. And I was suffering the consequences.

I hadn't realised how blind we can all be to the effects of Imposed Power until I started a project that looked at the question of language. This was a conversation I kicked off about the use of war words in business, politics and life called 'Make Words Matter'. I'd seen it first in a corporate sales environment when I noticed a sales director kept using the language of the battlefield to inspire her troops to go out into the field of conflict to fight off competitors to win customers. The brief for the project was simple. It was an investigation into the use of war words, the language of the world of imposition – fight, battle, troops and the like – in daily life. The question was: did people notice it? In the year or so that we actively pursued this project, I and the others engaged with it found out that very few people had. We also saw that even the limited number of people who'd noticed it hadn't really thought about it. This question tended to lead to a bigger and even more interesting conversation about whether the language was helpful or not. Generally, it seemed that once people thought about the language they and others were using, they realised there was something here that was worth thinking about more deeply.

The project kicked off after an event in Brighton, full of some of the most liberal, well-meaning people I had ever met. I was attending the 'Meaning' conference in 2016, where the co-leader of the Green Party, Jonathan Bartley, spoke passionately about the Government's policy on refugees at the time. The Greens had coordinated a humanitarian response asking for change. We all agreed that change was necessary. After calling for a line in the sand, Bartley told us that we had to 'go on fighting together as progressives', that we had to 'fight back', and that this was 'something we had to fight for very, very strongly'.

Previously, I'd sat listening to Jo Berry, whose father had been killed by the IRA in the Brighton bombing. Jo had gone on to not only forgive but meet the bomber, Patrick McGee, in order to understand him as a fellow human. Perhaps with this in mind, the irony of the language hit me hard. Jonathan's intent was positive and caring; he was also talking about being open hearted and having the need to achieve freedom for these people. However, at the same time he was using language steeped in coercion. Bartley was asking us to define ourselves by reference to oppressive force. He was asking us to rise up and fight against an existing system. This sat really badly with me. Ultimately, framing our actions as war results in us giving our energy away. Instead of putting our resources into being creative to build something new, we squander them in battle, handing the majority of our power to the other side and to the fight itself. It is the battle that then defines us: loser or winner.

Some of the most interesting conversations I have had about 'Make Words Matter' have been with the genuine soldiers I talked to. What they recognised was both the danger of any rush towards fighting as the best solution and the necessary precision of language. Because they had actually fought, they had experienced both the addictive pull but also the shortcomings of imposition as a model. For example, they talked about the importance of 'unsettling the moral will to continue' in their enemy rather than simply 'destroying' the other side. In the military, they had learned that war was a strategy rather than an aim in itself, that peace was the real objective, not the actual fighting. In that realisation, the language they used necessarily became more precise.

In these conversations, I felt like scales were falling from my eyes. As I began to see the fog of blindness that had engulfed me I also realised that this fog was widespread. Very few people, outside those with genuine experience of fighting, understood what the words they had fallen into using in their daily lives were really saying. The idea of war and fighting as a solution had been appropriated into the public arena without any agreement or discussion. We were unwittingly normalising psychological warfare into our everyday lives. People were now 'fighting' everything, from the new development in the village to the illness that was in their own body. I knew there was something bigger behind this.

Eventually, a film director came up to me in a workshop I held about 'Make Words Matter' and asked me to be clearer with my own language. At first, I did not understand. Then he explained. I had said the war language was being used metaphorically. He wasn't so sure. In his job, actors expected him to give them clear direction on their underlying motivation. Was the language of fighting really a metaphor, he asked me, or was it a lived reality? I had to think about it and eventually had to admit to him that my brain was already hurting with the question, and I didn't know. I had thought that the language of fighting was simply a metaphor. I didn't think people were actually fighting. He, rightly, challenged this assumption. What he saw was that it was not being used metaphorically. People were not saying it was '*like* fighting', they were saying that it *was* fighting.

I hadn't realised until this point that people were using the language of war and fighting because it captured the lived reality of how they felt. I realised how trapped I had been, and how trapped others might be. We weren't consciously choosing this language or the framework of power it sat within; we were enclosed in it. The coercive language of Imposed Power was embedded in the wallpaper of the room, framing any view of or from that room. This project about language helped all of us that were involved with it see just how we were stuck in a way of seeing, a reality tunnel where the prevailing model of power was so much part of the normal fabric of the place that we tended not to notice it. The project showed me how deep the problem was and that it wasn't just me who was caught up in it. The prompt was language, but the discussions soon went to wider issues. It was in these moments that I realised just how deep and addictive the trap was for us all. The walls were so high that it was genuinely difficult to see out.

It is not so much that Imposed Power is a bad strategy. It is more that we tend to follow it unwittingly. Occasionally, fighting does serve a purpose: sometimes we do have to defend ourselves and a clear reaction from the prevailing power system can serve to define a cause. This is something radical causes, in particular, tend to do quite effectively. Neither the IRA nor ISIS would be anything like so well known as they are without having a boost to their credibility given to them by those they set out to oppose. Sometimes, when we choose it for good reasons, fighting can be a good strategy; the problem is that most of the time we are not consciously choosing it. As 'Make Words Matter' showed, it is too easy to find ourselves having blindly adopted it.

The allure of warfare and the benefits of fighting in today's world are also largely mythical. When we think of warfare we tend to still think of something honourable in it. We see the warrior as noble. The truth is that ever since the soldiers who experienced the First World War came home we have started to realise that there is a deeper truth to warfare. The problem is that it is glorified in our films and in our culture. Some films are bloody, but even then it is rare for the popular filmmaker to dwell on the true human costs of war. In these films and images, we do not get to viscerally experience the human pain and suffering and the brutal efficiency of the modern depersonalised industrial killing machine that now does the job on the real battlefields of the world. In the wars that are now fought in the world people are killed with a machine approach on an industrial scale. The consequences of war are horrific. If we want to look at what war really is, we have to take the counsel of the soldiers and not just those who are excited by the prospect of heading off into war but those who have survived through it.

The illusions war creates run even deeper. In his book *The Warriors*, J. Glenn Gray, who fought in the Second World War for the US Army, reflects on the difference he sees between friends and comrades. As they share the uniting experience of war, comrades come together, often vowing to remain true friends forever. What Gray noticed was that outside the theatre of war, this kind of friendship consistently struggled to survive. Gray concludes that true friendship is different. Friends find themselves in each other by consistently supporting each other in their own growth, seeking good for the other. In comradeship, the self is sacrificed to the mission. Once that mission goes so does the illusion of friendship. The uniting power of warfare is a dangerously addictive drug that leaves a cold-turkey vacuum when it ends.

It is the agony of mass killing, the brutality of chemical weapons, the detached surgical precision of the drone and the long-term annihilation of the nuclear option that define a modern war. I find it difficult to make any helpful connection between the reality of this activity and the manner in which I might do something about today's refugee problem or conduct a sales campaign.


In the modern world, we can see that war and the fear it uses as its tool is no longer a good answer for how we solve our problems. To some extent we have realised this. Today's bigger problem is that the Imposed Power at the heart of the behaviour that causes us to go to war has found other ways to continue itself. This was brought home to me one day by my daughter when, at twelve years old, she returned home from school one day with a story.

'Daddy, I've worked out something,' she said.

'Really?' I said. 'Tell me more.'

She went on to explain that there are a number of schools in the town she goes to school in. It's a small town and she knows a lot of kids, all of whom go to school in different places and come from very different backgrounds. In one school she knew of, kids got beaten up in the back of the bus. She then started to tell me about an 11-year-old boy she knew to whom this has happened. What she had noticed, she said, was that other families, other kids were different; in another school, for instance, you probably wouldn't go in the bus. You'd be more likely to go in your parents' car. If you did go on the bus and get beaten up, your parents would probably get you a taxi, or maybe a chauffeur. She then told me that she'd worked out what this meant: there is one group of people who solve things with violence and another group of people who throw money at the problem.

The Imposed Power that Monkey originally grabbed for himself as his aim has, for many centuries now, been slowly undergoing a change. What started as a need for dominance in the form of force, the ability to raise an army or subjugate villages with fire, spears or guns, has now modernised itself. At some point, economic power also joined the fray as money stopped being simply a tool of trade and became a measure of power. The money needed to raise an army became power itself. After 1945 we passed a peak of warfare when we saw that the atomic bombs that finally ended the bloodshed of the Second World War are ultimately useless. In response to this and the growing peace movement, Imposed Power now finds itself with a different but equally compelling narrative base – money as power. It is this monetary power that has now become the overriding global doctrine.

So instead of soldiers and weapons, what Monkey's framework of Imposed Power now ultimately seeks is money. In this stage of global development, things are mostly done for economic reasons. In business, we evaluate decisions based on their having a sound business case. A supplier who might have a better solution for the environment will often lose a bid if they are marginally more expensive. In our own homes, much as it might be a good idea to grow our own food or buy a more expensive form of packaging that we can then reuse, the relative cheapness of the alternative shop-bought product or the single-use plastic can stop us. It is too easy to shop with our wallets and many good initiatives like these are refused simply because they don't wash their face economically, just as other ways of acting are promoted because they are more profitable. The narrative is an economic one and woe betide an argument that tries to buck the model.

The problem here is that whilst the gladiator of old had a dashing allure, there is less romance in pure money and the cynicism of its purpose becomes ever more apparent. The idea of a dominant warrior may have been attractive for a while but money itself can be grossly unattractive. Whilst a power system defined by money is better than one of war, many of us are now realising the fragility of a model that defines success simply as the attainment of power in the form of money.

Because we are living through this it can be difficult to step back from the action and to see what is going on. One man who did was General Sir John Glubb. Glubb served in the British Army from 1915 to 1956, mainly in the Middle East, and wrote a 1978 essay called 'The Fate of Empires'. What Glubb did in this work was to analyse the fate of 11 separate empires and to draw parallels between them. As well as finding that an empire lasts an average of 250 years, Glubb also found each empire went through the same six main stages. These are Pioneers, Conquest, Commerce, Affluence, Intellect and finally Decadence. The last empire Glubb looks at is the British Empire, which he plots in a cycle from 1700 to 1950 following the Ottomans from 1320 to 1570, Spain from 1500 to 1750 and the Romanov Russians from 1682 to 1916. Reading Glubb's essay it is easy to see that we have already lived through most of the stages of empire and that much of what we despair of in modern living can be put down to being in the Decadence stage. This is a stage where Glubb points out that frivolity and celebrity take over and political infighting intensifies. Reading his essay from the late 1970s provides a salutary reflection on where we are now.

One of the things Glubb's essay does is to strike a warning bell for the dangers that occur when money becomes the sole measure of any system. This is what happens in the final stage of Decadence, as more and more people take a self-serving behaviour into their own hands by gaming the system. Increasingly people grab money and power for themselves in a behaviour that inevitably fuels ever more desperation. It is also the case that today we all see these excesses more and more because we live in an increasingly transparent society. For example, when United Airlines simply chose to physically drag a passenger off an overbooked flight in April 2017 a large part of the world got to see the incident themselves on video. Power and wealth are ever more visible. We may aspire to a decadent champagne-fuelled lifestyle but we can also all see inside the lives of those who already have it more than ever. What is more, in this quest for the top, the problem with Monkey's original strategy of wanting to become the lion becomes obvious. We can also see there was only ever room for a limited number of lions.

The challenge with Imposed Power is that it is a pervasive framework that lives both in us and around us. It allows Monkey's original dominance strategy to be normalised and fear to prosper. We see it in the desire to impose on another that results in a voice being raised in conversation or a threat of a sanction being made. In that raised voice or threat, a Power Player has likely spoken, or a Standing Story been exercised. Imposed Power and the stirrings of fear it can engender are regularly used as an easy tool. The challenge in that moment is that both the existence of Imposed Power and its strategies tend not to be acknowledged. It is however a large part of what stops us as we struggle to quieten our voice in order to listen or to step back to adopt a more inclusive leadership style. Monkey's feat is to work so well with Beaver that the narratives and structures we hold onto that clothe our systems of power are invisible. Hidden, they more easily hold us.

What we've seen in the last two chapters is how something which starts as a successful strategy to solve a problem can easily become part of a bigger story. This narrative structure, like the crustacean's shell, tends to harden over time. The danger is that after a while we no longer see why that structure was originally created. The systems we work within, like Sue's ramp, make our lives easier, but our structures can also unwittingly re-enforce an overall framework of power that works by way of imposition.

Paul Gilbert, who now makes his living helping lawyers who work inside organisations, told me a story about how he saw the power structure show itself when he made a stand early on in his career for what he wanted. Paul had himself been working as the in-house lawyer in a large and successful building society. He'd been surprised when he got a job there initially but had been even more surprised when he got offered a promotion to the top job when his boss left. Paul didn't feel like he deserved it and had a severe case of imposter syndrome. Nevertheless, Paul took the top job and started to get on with doing it rather than worrying about it, something which he has always practiced, knowing how hard it is to shut off the voices inside our own heads.

One of the first things that happened in the new role was that the manager of the society's car scheme contacted him. Paul was eligible for a company car, and, it seemed, a rather nice one. Not only that, as a director, he was now allowed to park his new car in a reserved spot right outside the building. This would give him a guaranteed prime space at all times of the day and a spot where he could be assured of staying out of the wind and rain in bad weather. This was the sort of thing that one aspires to and Paul quite liked the idea of better parking. It would be useful in bad weather, at the very least.

The manager of the car scheme took Paul through his options and produced a range of glossy brochures. All the aspirational makes were here together with the reliable and trusty brands. Whatever Paul wanted was essentially on offer. This also wasn't just a case of having a nice executive car. Paul could have something even better, the sort of thing a director drove; almost the sort of car one might get driven around in by someone else. Paul took the brochures away in order to make his choice, and after a week of looking at all the various brochures and thinking about it, he spoke to the manager of the car scheme to give him his decision. Which shiny new toy would he like? Without really intending it, Paul was about to deliver a surprise. He asked the manager what was the simplest and cheapest car available that the company could provide.

'A Mini Metro,' replied the car scheme manager, 'But you won't be wanting one of those!'

The conversation with the incredulous manger went on for some time, but ultimately it was Paul's decision what car he got. He went away and thought about it, but his mind was already made up. He told the car scheme manager what he wanted, and soon he had his very own Mini Metro. He'd got a promotion he didn't expect and as a result of it he'd ended up with a car. It was a car that neither he nor his colleagues really expected. Nevertheless, it did everything that Paul could want from a car.

That, Paul thought, was the end of the story, but how wrong he was. Paul took to parking his car in the spot he'd been offered as a director, in front of the society's office. In between all the best of the prestige cars offered by BMW, Mercedes and the other top-end manufacturers sat Paul's Mini Metro, proudly holding, if not entirely filling, its spot. It wasn't long before Paul was pulled aside for a conversation with his boss, the CEO, who politely informed him that it wasn't possible for him to park the Mini Metro in the director's parking spot directly outside the building. Instead, Paul would have to park the car in the main car park, together with everyone else. Although Paul now had his choice of car, he wasn't allowed to park it in his allocated space.

It is in moments like this that we see how the overall system of power normalises itself. What has happened is that Monkey's original strategy has got so embedded into an overall framework that we tend not to notice. Like Paul, as soon as we start to do something different, we start to see that there are deeper forces at work. Not only is the power system present, it has also found a way to protect itself. Part of that protection is structural, but part of it is the hidden narrative structure that we all choose to promulgate about it. This is Beaver's work. Fear doesn't only exist, it also reinforces itself with the most powerful tool known to humans: the power of story. This story is something we all play our part in.

This has been the last part of our challenge – to understand Imposed Power and how it harbours fear. Because fear has had a fairly permanent berth in the docks for such a long time it is sometimes difficult to realise that both it and the harbour are man-made constructions. We only built the harbour to easily berth the ship. The problem is that as long as the port works okay we tend to be inclined to keep it going. What we don't always see is the cost of this. This includes the realisation that as long as we insist on keeping the harbour, fear will all too easily shelter itself inside it.

The good news is that there is another system of power altogether. This is where we will turn now, as we start to move into the positive question – what a new framework of power could look like and how fear might show up differently in that. If we want to make a shift and to build a new narrative, we may be surprised to see that this is something that we can reconnect to that we already know, rather than having to find something altogether new.

Where is the Imposed Power in your life?

# 6. Growth

On every journey, there are places we pass that we notice more than others. Some places make an impression on us that others don't. When we travel the same way again, some of these points persist and may even become markers by which we measure our progress. As we drive past a particular place we know how far we have come or have to go. As a child, I remember doing this on car journeys into London, as I stared out of the window, taking in the world beyond. I noticed the tower blocks off the dual carriageway and wondered about the people who lived in them, just as I always looked at the stall in the lay-by whose main product seemed to be potatoes by the sackload. Sitting in the car behind the glass window, these things called out to me as if they had a message for me that I'd yet to unravel.

Nowadays I still occasionally drive into London, sometimes as a passenger. I notice now that the level of attention I have for the world outside varies considerably depending on what else is on my mind. Sometimes I am in my thoughts; at other times, I am much more open to what is rolling by outside the window. Fortunately, I tend to notice the bigger things most of the time. One particularly notable point on my journey to the West End is a petrol station that sits on a junction. Late at night after an evening out, it is a joy to reach this milestone because I know home is one crucial step nearer. The junction marks a definite transition from the slower north London roads to a fast and open dual carriageway. I know that, from this point, things speed up.

A while ago I noticed that this petrol station was fenced in and closed. A few months later I passed and noticed that the forecourt of the station had been demolished. I started to wonder about its future. Recently, I looked out of the window again, as I went by after another short absence. Things were not as I expected. The development I presumed would happen on this pressurised spot of London real estate had not yet materialised. Instead the site looked abandoned. My immediate thought was that it was looking like a piece of scruffy overgrown wasteland. Then, as I looked more closely, I realised it was full of unexpected activity. White concrete was giving way to greenery as grasses and plants started to take over. New life was making its way up through the fractured ground.

I was curious about this, but it took a while before the significance of what I was seeing sank in. Suddenly I realised what it was. This small patch of land in the middle of an otherwise busy metropolis was reaching out to me as a reminder of what can happen when the forces of external development move out, leaving the earth to be. In the absence of an imposed outcome, it is not that nothing happens. Far from it. Instead, once the external actors lay off, we see life returning. Latent energy emerges from the ground. Shoots appear, seemingly from nowhere, rising up, finding their way through the cracks in the concrete. Before long, grasses and small shrubs make way for more persistent growth and small trees start to grow. In this once-busy place where we might have stopped to buy the fossilised remains of ancient trees in the form of liquid fuel, a green oasis of new trees and vegetation was starting to take over. The cycle wanted to come around. The pace may be different, but the site was busy again; a different sort of busy had been released from within the earth.

In today's built environment we are surrounded by things – phones, computers, TVs, abandoned games consoles, the knick-knacks that populate our houses, cars, roads and out-of-town shopping centres, all clutter our lives. It is easy to forget that however precious these things may seem to be, they have no life. In my days working for the big corporation, I'd often go for many days on end working on a project in a city somewhere, getting increasingly agitated. One night, I arrived late at night in Stockholm and was dropped off at my hotel from the airport by taxi. I should have just gone to sleep before a meeting the next day, but I knew that I didn't want to go straight off to bed. After checking into my room, I went out on the street at midnight. I didn't know why, I just felt the need to. Once I was there I found myself apologising to a city that I knew of old but now was just passing through. I felt I was ignoring an old friend and wanted to make what limited amends I could. As I stood looking at the stars in the night sky, I realised I was spending my life living inside a box, where all I ever saw was other people who were doing the same. As I stood there, my senses came alive. Even the frosty smell of night refreshed me in the way that no sleep would. I realised that there was a whole bunch of life, right here under the stars, that I was failing to connect with. It took me a little while longer to see that it was myself I was talking to, not the city.

I then realised that this night–time assignation with a street in the frozen night wasn't just a one–off waking up; it was a turning point. I knew I needed nature; I needed to connect with my own nature and to explore my connection with something bigger. From that starry night on, whenever I could I'd go walking with one of my team or a colleague in the park, often on the premise of solving a problem, but in reality, just to get out, to see life outside our little box and to reset our sense of what the possibility of being alive really consisted of. Surprisingly often, I'd find immediately measurable value in this as we'd see the problem we had in a different light. By these small measures, I started to move in a fundamentally different direction.

For a tree, life is metabolism, the process of staying alive. The origin of the word 'metabolism' is telling us of this in its derivation from the Greek word *metabole*, for change. The tree, like the plants growing on the abandoned site, simply lives, fulfilling its mission to be what it is capable of being, to the best of its ability, in the circumstances it finds itself. The tree is an ongoing act of becoming. As far as we know the tree has no consciousness. Trees therefore have no ability to question themselves and no conscious capacity to interfere with their own change or growth. The tree simply becomes the best tree it can be, given what it has.

In the 17th century René Descartes with his famous *cogito ergo sum* not only carved an ever–deeper distinction between thinking and feeling but also added to the frame of thinking built up over the centuries, which says that it is our thinking which defines us. This view has been much argued against but its central distinction persists as the Cartesian system of thinking named in his honour. Cartesian dualism insists that mind and body are separate, and in our world today the thinking brain continues to be the master. It is not surprising that we struggle to resist it. It is the wise counsel of our brain, after all, that speaks to us of its own supremacy.

We already know that our thinking systems are not really to be trusted. This is something Daniel Kahneman, the winner of the Nobel Memorial Prize in Economic Science in 2002, set out in his book *Thinking Fast and Slow*. Kahneman shows us how we really make decisions and has a model where he splits our thinking into two systems, one of which does the slow thinking and one the fast reactions. Even in this model of split thinking we know that most of our big decisions are made quickly and instinctively. If we can solve a problem easily, we will. Few of us really like using the highly energy-sapping space at the very top of our heads more than we need to.

If we applied this primacy of thought to the tree it would be very easy to arrive at a point where the only part of a tree we saw any value in would be the leaves. We might say that the leaves are not permanent fixtures, and we'd be right – but the same is true of our thoughts. These come and go just as the leaves do. Like our heads, the leaves act as a receptor and transmitter for a central organism which is far more complex but tends to be less obvious and quieter. In focusing on just the leaves we'd miss the root system, the capillary action that pumps moisture up to the leaves and the main engine room of the tree that turns carbon dioxide into carboniferous wood in the body. It is here, in the body of the tree, that the DNA of what makes the tree a tree is stored. If the leaves fall or a branch is cut, the tree will know to grow on. Just as the leaves are not the tree, our thoughts play a crucial role in our lives, but they are far from being the entire system.

The truth for our human bodies is not so different from that for the tree. Each is a system of many interconnected parts, and in both it is not obvious where the system ends or indeed whether it is separate at all. In language we define the tree and the person as separate things, which leads us to believe that each can disconnect from the system in which it operates, but in practical terms that is not so. The human needs the earth for even the basic things such as the air and water that sustain us. In space, we need oxygen to be shipped in and a life support system just as the plant taken into a house needs us to provide water and fertiliser. Below these surface needs, we are even more complex. Just as the tree depends on fungal growths to supplement its own root system, we can see it in our own reliance on the complex system of microbes that populate our guts – a system that we are still struggling to understand.

This tendency to live in and define ourselves by our thoughts puts us, we think, in a different position to plants and trees, but also mere animals who, we tell ourselves, do not think at all. Instead, having ascended beyond classifying ourselves as animals, we talk about whether or not animals are 'sentient beings', a term that has the danger of sounding like a label for a lower class of things completely. In order to distinguish ourselves as humans clearly from our ape forebears and other animals, this separation may have been necessary once but today seems like an ever-more-unfortunate divide from who we really are. Sentience really refers to a class of beings that have senses. This is a group to which we very much belong ourselves. We are not so different. Our ability to sense and to feel is a critical part, if not *the* critical part, of being human.

My expectation for the petrol station site was based on an assumption built in this world of modern thinking. Today we are used to ideas being mooted, plans being made in an architect's office, discussions being had, disagreements occurring, permissions being sought, a range of trades and professions being commissioned, materials being shipped in and an impressive development of the site to proceed apace. As we pass building sites we see deliveries arriving, scaffolds going up and coming down, workers busy and a building emerging. In this world of rationality and planning, what happens is that nature is held back and highly controlled. The power here is held externally and the construction that takes place is imposed on the site.

This is the choice that we have in any situation. When we walk into a room, we can either impose our views on others, or we can listen, observe and nurture what would come up naturally. If we can see an outcome, it is easy to find ourselves imposing that future on others. If we are rushed and stressed, under pressure to get things done, we may find it difficult to release our control over where we would like to take things. If we are fearful of failure, this pressure will add its own weight. If we feel the need to prove ourselves, then this in turn piles on the stress.

Nature's approach is entirely different. There is no thinking.

Instead, life just happens. Seeds are present somewhere in the soil, or they find their way in with the help of the wind or an animal. The seeds find the nutrition they need in the earth, the air, the rain and groundwater and, in the light of the sun, growth happens. The ancient Greeks were right: the basic elements of earth, air, water and fire, in the form of the sun, are all that are required for life. On the 'abandoned' site, the power is held internally, and what emerges is self-enabled. In both approaches, something with height and stature will appear on the site, but the methods themselves differ greatly.

Because the prevailing framework we live within is constructed and based in thought, it is all too easy to fail to connect to what our senses are telling us. As we travel, we may notice something as it passes by outside the window, but if our thoughts intervene, the sense that we feel in that instant may not be what we connect to. In a busy mind, there can easily not be enough space for the feeling we have to fully emerge. Then, because the framework we live within pulls us quickly onward, we have moved on. We find we have already travelled away from that moment of possible connection. Instead, we are now deeply buried beneath what new layers of thoughts are telling us. As this happens again and again, our senses give up. If you were trying to communicate with someone and they continually ignored you and moved on, wouldn't you also give up eventually?

In contrast, what the tree has is an abundance of sensing. It has no hearing, sight, taste or smell in the form that we might recognise, but it does have the ability to grow up towards the sunlight and to change its direction of growth in response to the direction the sunlight comes from. Microscopic mouth-like openings in the leaves, called stomata, open and close to regulate the passage of gases including carbon dioxide and water vapour. These close in response to signals sent from other parts of the tree, including the roots, which may send a signal up the tree that warns of impending drought. The tree networks this information and shares it around its system.

Trees and plants also have the ability in their branches and roots to sense and to respond to that sensing. They have something like our sense of touch. If a root of the small tree that now grows on the derelict site comes across a stone that forms an obstacle to its path in the ground, the tip of the root will sense the presence of that stone. Indeed, it is here where the tree keeps the seat of its intelligence, regulated by chemical messages. Instead of stopping to consider its options or arguing with the stone about the rights that each has and who was there first, the root will simply move round the stone. There is no debate about on whose side the law is likely to be or who might own the ground, the root simply senses the presence of the stone and moves on. In time, the root grows stronger as it travels on further in the ground, and as it grows its stronger girth pushes the stone out of the root's original path.

The tree has what the 12th-century Benedictine abbess and polymath Hildegard of Bingen called *viriditas*; the green growth that symbolises vital and verdant spiritual and physical health. This is the tendency that all life has to embrace its circumstances and to ply its energy to evolve into ever-more complex forms. The Abbess's observation is a theme picked up by the 'Green Man', an ancient symbol of nature of Greek and pagan origins that is still with us, albeit mainly in the naming of public houses, particularly in my native Essex. In this form, the Green Man lives on in name, but the connection to nature that he stands for currently plays very little role in our lives. The *viriditas* he represents has instead, particularly in the last millennium, been under continual threat as we have chosen to subjugate nature in our quest for efficient agriculture and better living standards. In making ourselves safer by warding off the bad, we have succeeded in losing connection with the bits of nature that are not only good for us but perhaps, like the air we breathe, essential. This conflict is picked up metaphorically in the 12th-century tale of St Amand, the seventh-century patron saint of vintners and brewers, who instructed a blind pagan woman, as part of her conversion to Christianity, to chop down a tree – an act which also restored her sight. Again and again, we see this story played out as we are encouraged to chop down the tree, both as a symbol and as a practical reality.

In contrast to the tree that innately finds its way, the development on the site is, at the same time that the vegetation prospers, in all sorts of trouble. The architect cannot get the client to approve the plans, the planners aren't happy with the proposed volume of the building and the construction is over budget. All these obstacles slow the project down as one person's thought faces another in a constant dance of possibility that could stop the project altogether. The energy of everyone involved in getting the building to be a financial and architectural success can easily end up getting buried in the details. Instead of that energy going directly into producing growth on the ground, it is in continual danger of being lost as it dissipates into a messy battle of wills. The system becomes one of opposition, as one thought opposes another.

On the building site, the focus is on an outcome. As observers, we may not know what the building will be, or the details of how or when it will be completed, but we do expect a result to be achieved. In order to reach this end goal, a myriad things need to happen along the way, and anything that slows down the satisfaction of any of these necessary steps is something that has to be dealt with and solved. Information that might take us down a different route tends not to be welcomed. What we tend to do is to push ever harder on towards our own imposed goal, rather than dwelling on what comes up. In order to get things done, different people take different approaches, but at the extreme, the driving project manager might ride roughshod over concerns that others might have. Where an objection has the legal or physical power to stop the development these may have to be acceded to, but others can be pushed on through, as the neighbour with a concern is placated, the tree is dug out or the lump in the ground gets broken up and bulldozed over. This is a builder who gets things done. As Machiavelli might have said, 'the end justifies the means'.

The more we look at the world of trees, however, the more we can discover about their surprising ability to adapt to circumstances and to create strategies. If we look at the branches of a beech or a silver fir and see that the tree is wider than it is tall, then we can tell that it is biding its time, waiting for conditions to change in its favour. In the meantime, it is extending its reach horizontally to gather what it can from the sun as efficiently as possible. These trees make choices. They are either on a growth spurt or playing a waiting game. Like all plants, the tree responds to changes in light conditions. This can result in simple behaviours, such as when a houseplant turns towards the sun, or the more sophisticated strategy we call 'photoperiodism', where plants respond to changes in the length of day and night to make choices about when they flower.

As well as being able to manage the small matters of size, diet and appearance, trees are surprisingly good at sex too. For us mammals, with legs to get us about and arms to cuddle with, sex is a pretty easy thing to achieve but if you are a tree, rooted to one spot, reproduction is substantially harder. Although plants have the option of simply cloning themselves, many do go to the trouble of mating with another, thus ensuring diversity. Their seeds may be dispersed on the wind or by animals, and their strategies for achieving pollination can be complex. These vary from the 750 or so types of fig which each team up with their own particular species of pollinating wasp to the bird cherry that blocks any lazy bee that seeks to bring its own pollen back. This damp-loving tree thus has a strategy that prevents it from inadvertently having sex with itself. That's not bad for a stick of wood that's stuck in the ground.

Trees also communicate, both with each other and with the forest around them. On the African savannah, umbrella thorn acacias haven't just learned to pump toxic chemicals into their leaves to stop giraffes from tucking into their feast. The trees also pass on the message that there are giraffes in the vicinity by releasing ethylene gas so that other trees know a predator is about. As a result, the giraffes have to move on completely or go upwind if they can.

In her 1997 scientific paper 'Mapping the wood-wide web', researcher Dr Suzanne Simard showed that mycelial fungal connections underground act in ways we are only just starting to understand. In her team's study of Douglas fir trees, Simard showed that trees don't compete like we tend to. Instead, the trees and their networks support each other. She found that not only are resources transferred from older trees to younger ones using the mycorrhizal network, but that old wood was best left in place to support this transfer. One older tree just outside the sample boundary was connected to 47 other trees in the 30-metres-square plot sampled, which implies it was also connected to many others outside the area. What Simard crucially showed was the reason why a transplanted tree stripped of its connections would suffer. Without the system of which it is a part, made up of other trees and the fungal connections established in the soil, the tree struggles, as we might also.

Perhaps most significantly, we think of the tree as an object that stays in one place. We know that trees can't walk, but the system a tree is part of can move in response to changes to the weather. The jay, one of nature's heavy lifters, tends to be the removal method of choice for the rather relaxed but persistent beech tree. With the jay's help, as a seed dispersal agent, whole forests of beech are consistently moving in central Europe right now. At the moment, they are marching north in search of melting ice at the rate of about a quarter of a mile per year.

Having read about some of the amazing things trees do, you may be wondering why we don't hear more about them. That is a good question to hold on to, whilst perhaps reflecting on how much of the nature programming we have traditionally seen tends to be focused on predatory animals. This is done for a reason. Programmers don't just give us what they want, they give us what *we* want. Stories of lions, bears and wolves tend to feature highly. If we find prey animals and the big animals more interesting than the trees and plants and the smaller animals, we might like to consider why that is. Our interests may well tell us something about our underlying default model of power.

That default model shows up in ways we barely recognise. For example, because of the way we tend to think, we rarely do a fair cost/benefit analysis of our actions. When we are faced with something that needs to be done, we do a benefit/cost analysis instead. What we tend to do is to weigh the benefits of fast, direct and thus imposed action against the costs of a more indirect, consultative approach. In doing that we miss or play down two other factors: the costs of an imposed solution and the benefits of a more open approach. We see certainty, speed and efficiency as the benefits of the directive approach lining up against the dangers of uncertainty, slowness and inefficiency. This is particularly true in an organisation where there are many people and moving parts involved. We take the clarity of conclusion against the chaos of consultation. That quick fear-based assessment often settles the question in favour of speedy, centralised and imposed action. In times of tension and war this is often referred to a precision 'surgical strike', an action which often seems logically attractive at the time, until we see its repercussions later.

This is, however, an unfair match. How can we allow ourselves to compare the best of one against the worst of another? In a fair contest, we'd bring in two more factors: the cost of the imposed approach and the benefits of the less directive growth-based model. If we did that, we'd see the options we have in a totally different light. Increasingly this is what organisations are starting to do as they explore the power that emerges when you become an enabler rather than an enforcer and give responsibility to a team to come up with ideas. This is a form of strategy workshop that genuinely asks the team for their ideas as input before deciding on the organisation's direction. When we do that we see the creativity that emerges and the long-term connection and ownership that the team gets over their solutions. Against this, increasingly we see the costs of a demoralised and perhaps slightly bullied and fearful workforce who are fed up with being told what to do and have stopped taking any responsibility for the outcomes of their daily work. By looking at these factors we could start to do a realistic cost/benefit analysis of our actions in the first place. If we did that we'd see more clearly what we already know but struggle to admit – we may have less control, but people perform better when we distribute power and instil responsibility.

Jim Walsh is the CEO of the Conway Hall Ethical Society, an organisation which is unusual in that it is both a promoter of free thought itself and a provider of a venue that encourages action in that regard. Jim came to our very first fear workshop and it is thanks to him that I ended up running workshops at Conway Hall. Jim is a philosopher, and over a lunch in my early days of running the workshops I managed to drain him of ideas whilst putting the world to rights. As the lunch came to an end, I started to call us both out by saying that all our talking was all very well but action was surely required. Jim agreed and suggested I went and talked to James Hillhouse. James works in the ad industry and is the co-founder of an agency called Commercial Break. I managed to meet James for an indulgent late breakfast in an old warehouse in King's Cross and was immediately struck by not only the strength of his ideas but also the challenges he was having in implementing them. This contrasted with the genuine understated brilliance of what the agency he started has achieved. What James is doing is to nurture an inner voice that reminds me, at the same time, of the source of core energy I saw emerging from the ground on the building site, on which plant and tree life depends.

The idea for Commercial Break came from a project James carried out for the Metropolitan Police. The Met's question was about Crimestoppers, a hotline run in the UK to encourage the public to provide anonymous information to help the prevention or investigation of crime. The hotline has been a success for many years, but the Met could see that it was coming up against limits in a world driven not by the logic of reporting a crime but by questions of trust in the system. People weren't phoning in as they had been doing.

As he was an experienced advertising consultant, the question the Met had for James was: 'Will young people phone Crimestoppers?' James was confident he could find out and when he got the project he duly set off to answer the question. However, at the end of the project, as he delivered the answers to the Met and to its various advisory groups, he realised that what he was saying lacked authenticity. As a relatively privileged white guy, not really from the target group, he could provide answers as he saw them but he could also see that wasn't really getting to the root of the issue. The truth was that the young people he was interviewing were the real source of the answers. In reporting back, he was being largely being a mouthpiece for these young people. James slowly came to the realisation that what he should have done was to ask the Met not to employ him but to instead employ kids themselves to answer the question. The question was after all addressed to them, so who better to answer it? This idea became what is now Commercial Break.

What Commercial Break does is to work on one project for one client every year. Its clients are big names like Dr Dre, ITV, EE,

UbiSoft and Comic Relief. What all of these big organisations want is to understand what their young consumers are really thinking. Every year Commercial Break brings a team of six to ten young people together on a chosen project and then lets them loose. There is no adult who comes in to sanitise this – everything comes direct from the kids, who often end up delivering some hard messages, effectively calling out the emperor's new clothes directly to the emperor.

Commercial Break's clients get not just insights into what young people are thinking, but also ideas and solutions. For example, Comic Relief were struggling to get donations from young people and asked for help in solving the problem. What the Commercial Break team told Comic Relief was that texting a donation, an idea introduced to make things easier, was actually still more difficult than it needed to be. One of the Commercial Break team said that what she'd like to be able to do was to be able to tell her iPhone to donate and for that to happen. This struck a chord and from that observation she went on to develop an idea where you could tell Siri to do the setting up of the donation for you. All you now have to do is to say that you want to donate to Comic Relief or Red Nose Day and the donate window is opened in your browser; then you simply confirm the amount of the donation. As a result of this insight, donating got easier, particularly for the younger audience.

As he worked on developing Commercial Break, James started talking to more and more kids, particularly the underprivileged ones, the majority of whom came from what we call racial minorities, who lived in the run-down inner-city housing estates, where a lot of crime was being committed. He found that these young people had a highly polarised way of thinking about their futures. They saw themselves as either making it really big, in becoming the next celebrated rap star or, alternatively, working for a pittance in a local retail chain with no prospects. The power model had them either as superstars up high, or victims down low. What James realised as he talked to them was that there was no realistic middle ground which took them into the world of work that could even start to fulfil their largely untapped potential in an effective way.

As James talked, I could see that providing this lifeline had become his passion and the root of the new agency's mission. Commercial Break now works with kids in the most underprivileged positions, who have something to offer but who need someone to give them the opportunity to express it. James looks for raw talent that has gone un-nurtured, and has found a way to work with individuals to help them to grow. He has a knack of seeing and enabling pure potential. Rather than imposing a solution on these young people, James helps them to take realistic steps forward from where they are that take account of who they are.

James cites a project Commercial Break did with ITV to be one of his most satisfying pieces of work. The team worked on the MOBOs, an awards ceremony started in 1996 specifically for 'music of black origin', and came up with the idea of a 'Paving the Way' award for an artist who does exactly that for the next generation. Part of the idea is that the chosen artist gets to choose where the paving stone that is the award should be placed.

Wiley, who is often called the Godfather of Grime, won the award in 2015, in its first year, and chose to have the stone cemented on the path towards the assembly hall in the grounds of the Tower Hamlets school he and his father both attended. When he spoke to the children at the school he busted the myth that success just happens, when he talked of the long journey that he had to go on to achieve what he has. A classroom full of admiring kids were left in no doubt about the tens of thousands of hours of work and the love and passion they would each need to have to go on a similar journey themselves. Crucially, Wiley's stone contains the words 'I'm so E3, the whole of E3 got so much talent, I hope you see' from his song 'Bow E3' as an homage to Wiley's roots.

As James and I talked, this concept of 'roots' and their importance came up consistently. At one point, I even summarised what he said by putting the idea into a form of words – 'Don't go from the branches, go from the roots!' This is the challenge we have in modern corporate life; it is all too easy to go for the quick fix, a small, token change that looks like it addresses the problem, but is actually up in the cosmetic branches.

In response to this, James told me about some of the things Commercial Break notices as they try to place their candidates in established agencies in long-term jobs. The problem is that not every employer provides a similarly nurturing environment. In particular James told me a story about a talented young woman he'd championed who'd left the agency she'd been placed in. She'd been welcomed in initially but hadn't felt this was somewhere she'd wanted to stay. I was interested why that was. The particular part of the story that struck me was that she'd arrive on Monday morning and found that the conversation was essentially about *Downton Abbey* and Waitrose. Her weekend had mostly been spent with friends at a late-night warehouse party, an impromptu gathering in an as-yet-unfinished penthouse flat. Over time, she declined to fit in with the prevailing discussion topics and noticed that very little interest was shown in the alternatives she might contribute. As a result, she felt more and more like an outsider. This process of fitting in happens to all of us to some extent. If we want to be a part of an organisation as it is, we all tend to compromise and often homogenise ourselves into the whole. In this process, we can lose what marks us out. Not everyone, however, particularly today, is prepared to compromise like this. This was an organisation that embraced diversity, as most do nowadays, but at the same time, couldn't provide nurture for this young person's roots.

Part of the problem here is the same one as I had when I found myself standing outside my hotel in Stockholm. This is that we don't know what our roots really are. A combination of what we know and what we fail to sense stops us from seeing what is right in front of us. Thus, as a 21st-century human being it is all too easy to be confused. I blame Monkey for this. What Monkey has done has given us the idea that we are simply a smart ape. As a result, we tend to see ourselves as an advanced version of him. If we continue to do this, it's not surprising that we struggle to lose many of our ingrained habits, including those that give us our fear. Do we want to stay a smart ape forever? That might be alright for some but, frankly, I don't trust some of his antics.

Instead, we could look at what our bodies really are and appreciate the evolution that they are actually the result of. Life on earth started in bacterial and cellular form and has been in that form for most of earth's history. Life eventually evolved through plants, fish, reptiles and then, most recently, into mammals. Far from being the origin of life, Monkey is a relatively modern branch. This means that the lessons we have to learn from evolution and our connection to it, our roots, go far deeper. Counting cells in our body is a hard thing to do, but there are thought to be as many as 50 trillion of them, mostly working in cooperation. That is a lot – thousands of times more than the 7.5 billion people on earth. In addition, the bacteria in our body outnumber the cellular content on a ratio of something like 10:1. If we are looking for connection to life we should be looking more towards the cellular, bacterial and plant end of life than we do. It makes sense that the great outdoors has a lot to teach us. We have lessons to learn from all of life, not just a few predators. This stuff is what we are made of, not bits of Monkeys.

To be fair, apart from the paranoid fear bit, the prevailing Monkey narrative has done a great job for us. It got us here. The downside of it is only becoming more apparent now. This is that it disconnects us from the wider system of nature of which we are a part. As a result, more and more of us are now seeking to reconnect with nature. My own personal favourite pioneer in this endeavour is early ecologist and writer John Stewart Collis. After a long hard day working in an ash wood in Sussex in the 1940s, Collis sat back in a blissful state reflecting on his utter joy. Collis, who'd been employed to clear and thin the wood, started to make the connection to what is needed. What Collis realised in a moment of clarity was that there is no need to search for anything. What he saw was that he was already in the Garden of Eden. He writes that there was no error in speaking of the Garden as existing but there was an error in tying it down to time and place. He remarks in his book *The Worm Forgives the Plough* that all we need is the key to the gate to access it and concludes:

'...at the birth of consciousness, we became onlookers and were separated from nature, and left the garden to create a world of our own apart from Nature. Our next step is a further extension of consciousness when we shall realise the unity of life on a higher plane of understanding. Having tasted of that tree of knowledge we shall enter the Garden of Eden once more and Paradise shall be regained.'

What Collis identifies is that the path to reconnection exists already. This is an Eden which can be re-entered. In order to do so all we have to do is to open up to a direction of travel towards, rather than away from, the richness of our own nature and that of the world around us. The beauty is that the model for this is already at hand. However, it requires us to learn not just from the predators which we have directly usurped but also the lessons of the more ancient and formative forest and the cellular and biological life that has been there all around us, providing our oxygen for living, all along.

The change here from Monkey is that what we now seek is connectedness and unity. This is about seeing ourselves as part of the whole rather than simply the top dog, able to play with nature as we like. It is a direction of travel that requires awareness of the forces of fear and story that originally separated us, driving us to believe that we needed control over our destination, promising us the shining false god of certainty of outcome. This is no longer about getting to a place – this is about already being here. It is about connecting to what we have and appreciating it fully.

This may feel like a new narrative, but its seeds are already there. The Welsh phrase *dod yn ôl at fy nghoed* is taken to mean 'returning to a balanced state of mind', but the literal translation is 'to return to my trees'. Even in language, though somewhat hidden, our true nature lives on.

In Chapters 3 and 4, in the Monkey and the Beaver, we met the forces that take us into a hostile, divided and fearful environment. We then saw these coming together in Chapter 5 as Imposed Power. In this chapter, we have seen that that there is something already here, in us, that exists in the roots of who we really are. As I found, the building site has an energy already, but we tend to not see this power when we build our imposed constructions over it. It is now time to explore this rooted power further and to meet some different sources of energy. The forces that come together to nurture this alternative approach are based, like those we've seen in this chapter, not on imposition but on growth.

What part of the natural world do you feel most connected to?

# 7. Our Fear Friend

My secondary school prided itself on its careers advice. The teachers, who perhaps weren't the most independent judges, even said it was 'the best careers office in Suffolk'. We pupils had our own crude version of this description, but in some ways it was true. The careers department did have its own elegant Victorian sash-windowed bright-white painted room upstairs in a distant wing. This gave our futures a detached aura of a serious world beyond school. Frankly, for us pupils, it was a place to be avoided, until it could be escaped no longer. We knew that finally, under duress and heavy adult direction, we'd be forced to pay a visit to this doctor's waiting room without a doctor. Here, the main attractions were the brochures so kindly provided by employers, waiting for us in racks on the walls like choice destinations in an old-fashioned travel agent's shop.

Much as the elevated white room holds memories, it is a talk given in an upstairs classroom in the main block of the school that lingers still in my mind today. The talk was given by the teacher who had the job of running the careers office, who we called 'Mouldy Meyers'. Mr Meyers taught French and talked to us one fine afternoon about flexibility. I remember his talk more than anything else I was ever told about careers by anyone, anywhere. What Meyers said was that the key thing we all needed to be able to do was to be flexible, and that the future belonged to the people who could flex to whatever life offered them instead of seeking to stay in one place. Unfortunately, what I remember is not what Meyers said in detail, but rather how we kids, at the time and for years after, ridiculed Meyers and the whole idea.

I suspect that the reason we ridiculed what was said was not that we thought it was fundamentally wrong, but rather the incongruity of the message coming from a teacher whose nickname alluded to the fusty character we saw. His point was well made but utterly clashed with what we thought of the man and the system he represented. If perhaps the talk had been given by someone who clearly practiced the art of flexibility, a circus performer with previous as a bank robber perhaps, we might have been more impressed. 'Yeah, stick it to you, best careers office in Suff\*\*k!', we might have said. Instead, 'flexibility' was a hypocritical afterword for me for years after that still smelt of Mouldy Meyers and the useless world of school careers advice.

Now, some 30 years later, I can see that not only was Meyers making a great point that day, but also that my reaction, part of our collective reaction to it, was much more revealing than the message itself. What I am struck by now is a memory of the hostility we had to the idea at the time. Our reaction speaks to the dark void that exists between what we say and what we do, which we tend to excuse by ridiculing or attacking others. The fault is right here, with us, but we'll do anything we can to avoid talking about that. Anything is better than allowing the focus to turn in, on ourselves. We run miles out of our way to avoid this straightforward challenge, and yet it is here that all our opportunity for growth lies.

Again and again I see that there is a significant delta between my nodding acceptance of a reality and my ability to act on it and do something different as a result. No idea I have matters, no thought I think matters, no statement I make matters and no thing I know really matters unless I enact it, and yet I can so easily continue to think that believing something is enough. It is self-help's critical weakness. We attend events and we read books, but very few of us change what we do day to day. If I enacted everything I agree with that I have heard and read, I would be living a completely different life.

This is the key challenge. I did take on board what Meyers said that day, yet in my lived life itself I have routinely ducked and avoided it. I have all too often simply gone with what seemed right, taken the structured usual answer, often following the easy money. The problem is that in this model, we don't tend to talk much about the things that really stop us. Indeed, these undefined monsters have a habit, if we let them, of pinning us down. At the extremes, a wall of fear can engulf us. We feel like we are helpless, in the claws of a predator. Our instincts are to freeze and to hide if we can. Many of us, particularly the more naturally introverted, might run to the bathroom or anywhere private, away from them. This can happen because we are facing a particular situation in the moment or it can happen more subtly.

What happens to us more usually is that we have an ongoing fear of something we know we need to do but which we are not facing. Our strategy becomes one of avoidance. Instead of being there, facing the tiger, we are simply taking alternative routes, 'pussyfooting' our way around the thing we fear.

Avoidance is exactly what I did for years as I clung on to a well-paid job and steadfastly refused to move into the next stage of my life. Instead of doing anything about the call I felt, I bought a sketch-book and wrote down in it everything interesting that I encountered, every idea, every wisdom. Rumi's classic poem 'The Guest House', an encouragement to seeing good in everything, however bad, that is sent to us, is an early entry. I kept the opening page to the notebook free and over time a series of quotes that had real impact for me even-tually gathered until the page was full. Here was Voltaire's 'doubt is an uncomfortable condition, but certainty is a ridiculous one', Lee Clow's 'The facts of the matter are rarely the heart of the matter', and Kafka's 'Anyone who keeps the ability to see beauty never grows old'. I had these thoughts, but the truth is I did little if anything substantive about what they were telling me.

The act of buying this perfectly designed red sketchbook was, however, in hindsight a crucial turning point. I was starting to hear something in me as it connected with things it saw in the world. Instead of running on a never-ending hamster wheel to somewhere that never arrived, I started to feel, to listen and observe more. I slowly got an emerging sense of connection, a growing relationship with what was really going on, primarily inside me as the signals them-selves responded. It felt that the more I listened, the more the feelings I had spoke up. When the real opportunity to jump came some years later, even if I didn't know that I was ready, it was as if readiness now lay in wait, inside me, waiting for a trigger.

I remember in particular one day as I arrived early in the morning at the offices of a new organisation I had now joined in a change of jobs. It was based in a gleaming glass tower with a huge marble reception and a bank of lifts to whisk one up to the offices beyond. As I got in the lift I felt my pulse quicken, preparing me for what lay beyond. As I connected what my body was telling me I realised that I knew something lurked in the corridors and heavily designed meeting rooms of the building that made me feel uncomfortable. Even the air in here was heavy. I may have been a director in the organisation, but I could still feel the presence of authoritarian power leaching out of the place, placing its tentacles around me ever more tightly as the lift ascended.

Whilst I was still in the lift, my body had told me something my brain didn't want to hear. This was not somewhere I wanted to be, this life was not healthy for me, and much as I cared for many of the people here, this was not an environment that fostered a sense of caring. I'd just gone through another turning point. However much I put it off, I knew now that this was not going to last, however much I fought that knowledge logically. This was the job I subsequently left; my last real 'job'.

From the notebook I also indirectly found an emerging willingness to experiment, to do things and to take risks. I went to more external events and met different people. I saw that I was not crazy. It was out of this that my confidence to engage in bigger change and experimentation eventually re-emerged. As time went on I did more things and experimented whilst watching my reactions and feelings. I saw that some things I tried out did work whilst others didn't. I started to accept the failures as part of the whole and to embrace and learn from everything. I started in a quiet way to take on my fears. It got easier to see what they were as I became more interested in them. At some point, I saw how I was being too conditional, waiting for others. I noticed how my reluctance to commit seeped into everything and stopped me taking a risk in anything. Unless I was prepared to be an anchor for myself, I wasn't ever going to get anything to work.

I wanted to set up a networking group for all the commercial people I knew in our business. I wasn't doing it because I was scared if I set something up no one would come. It also wasn't part of my 'job'. In the corporate structure, it was too easy to focus on the things we were told to do rather than pushing ourselves to do anything out of the ordinary or anything that was more self-inspired. There was no obvious advantage in taking those sorts of risks. Eventually, because it itched at me, I did it anyway. I organised a drinks evening in a bar. When the day came, I grabbed a colleague after work. We then sat in the bar for an hour with a bottle of wine desperately keeping the conversation going before one person turned up. Fortunately he was highly supportive and we had a good chat, but all the time while I sat there trying to focus on what he had to say I was gutted that no one else had turned up. Undaunted, I organised another drinks date and told everyone how well the previous one had gone. For someone like me, who could be 'glass half empty', this didn't feel true, but I told myself this was just perspective, and that for a 'glass half full' person it could easily be justified.

At the next event, I sat for half an hour on my own with a bottle of wine defending the table I had in the hope more people would turn up. It was almost as if life required me to learn the lesson of being able to order a big bottle and to sit there waiting to pour it. Eventually a few people did arrive. This second meeting was hard, but I didn't give up. I learned that often the second or third running of some-thing new is the hardest and sometimes all we need to do, after the initial energy of the first running, is to get through this difficult stage. The networking meetings continued on a regular basis and the num-bers slowly grew. Instead of assuming it should work and then being disappointed when it didn't immediately, I started to listen to what people said and to ask more questions. I slowly found out just why this was difficult for others and began to see how I might make com-ing along easier. All most people needed to know was that this was a long-term thing with some sort of a useful purpose. This was a thing I could solve. I also saw everyone else's fears and anxieties. I realised that it wasn't just me who was scared to do anything new. I saw fear in people from whom I wouldn't have expected it.

Most importantly, I learned that I could sit alone and wait if I had to. People would come if they saw I had commitment. The most important thing I learned was that once I started to take on my fears, those fears were nothing compared to what I thought they were. Fear was at its peak when I was a stationary captive, pinned down by it. I also noticed there were two types of creative people; those who got pissed off that what they wanted to happen didn't happen and those that just quietly learned from what happened and got on with it. I could see that something tried to propel me into the former category, but that in my soul I'd be a lot happier if I could dwell more in the latter.

Just as I had a fear that no one would turn up to the networking evenings, I had a similar fear that kept me from becoming self-employed. Would anyone turn up to that? Over time, I learned that this also depended as much on how I felt about myself as it did on almost anything. If I knew what I was going to do and committed to it, then, just like with the drinks, others would too. Not only that, I had to show that I was committed by not just having one event and expecting everyone to turn up. I had to stay with my commitment even when no one turned up. It was only then that people would know that I was serious and that the thing was definitely going to happen.

The most compelling fear I had when I left my job was about income. Because I had a salary of a certain amount I thought that I needed to find a way to replace that. This, I realised, was the biggest block of all, because it felt both certain and irreplaceable. It was certain because I never doubted its continuance, even though it was far from certain in other respects, as I could have lost my job at any time. And it was irreplaceable because I could never see myself selling enough of myself to make up for it.

When I made the jump for real I realised that everything was nego-tiable. First, I could find ways to survive without this income. This partly involved my own spending habits. If I stopped buying so much stuff, I suddenly didn't need so much income in the first place. Next, I could be more creative with how I did things. I could ask more favours and blag more stuff. If I waited and asked, things had a habit of working their way out that involved less or no money. Instead of using money to fix things, I started to look for other solutions. Slowly, what seemed impossible while I was afraid to jump became possible once I was in motion. It was ironic, but having no money to throw at things actually made me more creative, which in turn gave me power of a different sort.

Being in active relationship with what life offers us rather than imaginative paralysis does seem to help to put fear in its place. The main thing we do in a Fear Hack is to get into conversation, in relationship with, our fears and anxieties, instead of being pinned down by them. We make fear our friend rather than our adversary, and we do that in a supportive, safe way; we seek to be in the green zone of the traffic light. We have found that once we start to have an open conversation, our fears have something to tell us. Just like anything else, our problems shift once we understand the full picture. After this breakthrough moment, with sudden access to greater knowledge, we make realisations about what might now be possible.

In practical terms, it helps to have a constructive attitude to how we make this friend and how we treat it. Our anxieties are part of us. We wouldn't tell our leg to get lost. Like any part of our body, it helps to accept that our fears are there rather than ignoring them. Expecting them to go away or immediately trying to impose some other, more desirable, outcome of ours on them tends not to work. Instead, we want to welcome them. Ultimately, we want to make fear our tail-wind rather than having it blowing us backwards all the time. The problem is that we generally start off with our wind of fear blowing directly in our face. Expecting it to change direction by 180 degrees, when it's blowing against us, is a big ask. The answer to this is that it is we who have to accept the biggest change by accepting that the wind is as it is. We are like a sailor who has to accept the conditions as they are but has also worked out that they don't always have to be blown downwind. We learn that we can skipper our boat into the wind by first moving backwards and forwards across the wind, to get the measure of it, and then starting to sail more directly into it. Before long, we are able to use a headwind by tacking first one way, then the other, into it. Once we have mastered this it doesn't matter which way the wind is blowing, because we've worked out how to sail into it when we need to.

One of the exercises we do in a Fear Hack workshop is the 'Fear Dig'. In this people get in pairs to help each other to dig away at what is beneath what they see on the surface. We ask a simple series of questions that seek to dig down further into what we find, such as 'What is really going on there?' and 'What will happen then?' or just 'And...?' What we are looking for is what lies beneath the surface. We want to know what really drives the belief that we can see.

If someone is scared of leaving the house we ask what they think will happen when they do. We then ask about the worry they have of having to talk to the neighbour, and then what is beneath that. This is a simple exercise, but very few people have ever done it before, either for themselves or with a partner. Often having a partner is the breakthrough because the partner sees things that they have never seen. Suddenly an independent perspective is introduced and the mind is caught out. In this moment, we might see that a fear that has been earnestly held for some time is ridiculous.

Alternatively, there might be a realisation that we are overlooking a more practical element of our preparation, which is quietly bugging us, sitting beneath our everyday radar. Perhaps if we are worried about giving a presentation on an important occasion, we might know subconsciously that an element of our material is just not as good as the rest. We know that it is only by getting on our feet and practising it that we will see the flaw and discover a solution. But because we are not facing what our fear is telling us, we might not be doing the preparation we really need to do. We can be complicit with our fears. In this unspoken deal, we can end up allowing what we fear to prevent us from doing anything. This seems to solve it and we can end up believing that not facing the devil at all is the best approach. Unfortunately, it takes more than us wearing a blindfold to disappear the devil. While we are hiding behind the mask, the devil is busy growing. Sooner or later the fears will pop back up. If we run away from them, they generally become ever bigger as they chase us. If we walk forwards with them, they start to talk to us, to tell us things. What we are doing is starting to treat fear like a road sign, a signal that says to that something important for us lies in this direction.

In a Fear Hack workshop, we often go further by ending up with an exercise that takes us all the way to true friendship. This is a conversation between ourselves and our fears. Instead of having an internal conversation between parts of our own mind, we get to externalise the dialogue so that we can see what is going on. To do this, a small group of people get to be our fear so that we don't have to be it ourselves. Once we have explained what our fear is to two or three other people, they start their questions and observations with the words 'As your fear...' These people can then play our fears back to us. Once they get outside our own head, they tend to expose themselves for what they really are.

What these conversations explore is essentially how our fears get their energy. We realise that there are things that our fears want us to do and things that they don't want us to do. Our fears have strategies that hide but are there to be discovered. If we fear other people, our fear might want us to lock ourselves up at home. We might see that same fear also conspires to make us busy, taking on tasks so we can't make even the easy social engagements. By making us busy, our fear completes its strategy and gets its energy. We can reduce the energy our fear has by seeing this and recognising that we can do something about it. As this realisation breaks, we get bigger and our fear smaller.

Through exercises like this, we see that although we can make fear our friend, it's not really that fear is a good friend. In truth, our fear is mostly a bad friend; one who wants us to stay in a hole with them. This character I call our 'drug dealer friend'. This is the friend who is there for us but fundamentally wants us addicted to our fears. This can mirror real-life situations where, surprisingly, some of those we believe are our closest friends are not keen for us to change. If we changed, they might have to face up to things they don't want to face up to either. It is through this secret deal that a pair of long-term drinking buddies support each other in their continuing addiction. But it is in this open conversation with a known double-faced 'friend' that we learn most about how we contribute to our fears. When we ask, 'how can I help my fear to be stronger?' we tend to get revealing answers. When we ask what our fears most want, we see what we do that feeds them. Once we see that, we can also see how we can cut off that food supply. It is often the constant back-door feeding we do that sustains our fear.

The truth is that our fears only have power over us for as long as we resist them. It is our resistance that gives them energy and a reason to be. As Carl Jung said, 'What you resist will not only persist, but will also grow in size.' If we choose to be comfortable with the discomfort of our fear, letting uncomfortable be, it will cease to be uncomfortable. It is only by accepting the negative in the *dis*-comfort that it will lose its negative definition and cease to be the problem we see it as. What is more, it is a general principle that letting something be in turn lets us be. Instead, we can remake the relationship with our fears in a different frame of reference: that of friendship and growth. Once we put our arm around it, fear in the green zone of the traffic light feels different from how it does in the fight state of amber.


The problem Monkey has is that he doesn't get this. He is still terrorised by the lion and will always want to fight fear in the hope that he'll beat it. What he doesn't understand is that he is more usually subsumed by it. In this reframing exercise, what we want the Monkey to do is not to change (he probably never will) but to be quiet and to leave us alone. To do that it helps to replace him with a different metaphor. The one that seems to work here is of a horse. The relationship between people and horses is one that has been mutually beneficial to both over a significant period of our history, after all. All we are doing here is starting to see our relationship with our fears as a process of building a partnership that mirrors the relationship a long-term rider might have with their ride. Somebody, when they first saw the horse thousands of years ago, had the wisdom to get on it and to ride it rather than to fear it. The horse thus became man's particular friend rather than being just another wild animal. For most of us, the back of a horse is still not the most comfortable place to be, but we know that through working together through discomfort with a friend, we can challenge each other and get to some interesting places.

My own Horse of fear came into my life when I kicked off the networking group. As I decided to get on with the task my fears didn't go away, but I did start to understand and work with them better. As time went on I felt more confident, and this gave me a basis for taking on the next project. Now when I do the next thing I have a much stronger sense that I can ride through it and that the relationship I have with my fear is more manageable and more useful. Confidence can't be grown in a jar. We get it as the by-product of riding our fears through events that scare us. We may have the feeling of fear, but the good news is that we are actually riding it. And by riding it, we are moving forward and learning to ride it even better.

The other realisation we come to in the conversations we have is the reluctant acceptance of something we've quietly known all along. This is that there is an element in what we call fear which is an uncomfortable constant, and it's a constant that we have to learn to live with. It's a bit like being in the saddle, perhaps; some of us might get used to it, but for others it will always feel a bit uncomfortable. The trick is to realise that this feeling is normal and not to run away from it.

While I was in the closing stages of holding down a job in a big corporate I found myself in a situation which made me uncomfortable but also showed me why I needed to stay with it. I'd very kindly been invited to a three-day event in an old disused sail loft in the old docks in Copenhagen. Finally, the day arrived, and after being dropped off by a cab in the middle of nowhere I got lost between a series of vast warehouses. Surely, I thought, I must have this wrong. Eventually, my sense of direction switched on and, after turning a few corners, I found the place. It almost seemed as if it was hiding, as if too cool to sign itself, a couple of storeys up, off a secluded, derelict courtyard. Standing below, looking up at a half-derelict wall festooned with out-crops of wild flowers, I saw there was an old wooden door hanging off the wall and an old ladder you had to dare yourself up. 'Really?' I thought, 'Do I have to?'

Inside, the building was just as stylish as it was outside. There were workspaces behind glass, full of artisan treasures so creatively compelling that I simply couldn't take it all in. Everything looked like it came out of some unobtainable Nordic design aesthetic. Somehow the place carried decades of earnest distress whilst exuding a sense of youthful and vibrant creativity. The style factor didn't stop there. As I started to meet my fellow attendees, I was conscious they were different from the people I usually hung out with. They were actors, performance artists, writers, musicians and artists. I felt like a complete outsider and my sense of being completely lost continued.

The build-up to the event hadn't helped. It was called the 'Industrial Smorgasbord', and it was organised by one of the colleges of Oxford

University. It was of course intended to be wonderfully welcoming, and it was, but I didn't see it that way. As I read the profiles of all the participants on the event's wiki page I felt awed by their achievements in the world of the arts, drama and the creative industries. When it came to filling my own profile in, I left it for weeks, completely unable to think what I could say about myself that remotely measured up to what I'd seen. How did I ever get invited? Had they made a mistake? I wondered what right I had to be here.

Fortunately, I knew a couple of the other participants and slowly got to meet a few more. As I met people and talked to them, I started to realise that I wasn't such an outsider. Although the T-shirts a couple of the guys were wearing were like nothing I'd ever seen, these were people just like me, with concerns and worries just like I had. In particular they were trying to work out the commercial application of their work, which was entirely my experience and something on which I had a perspective. Slowly and by a series of breakthroughs, I started to see how I could relate to what was going on and, in time, how I could contribute. I started to relax and to get into some sort of a stride. When I did that things really started to open up. By the last day I even offered to run a workshop and took a small group outside to gather some thoughts on the topic of listening.

Over the few days that we were in Copenhagen we explored various creative formats. We danced, made shapes, drew, went and found things in nature, acted and even treated what we ate, and how we ate it, as a performance. Everything we did stretched me beautifully and, like a cat in the sun under a kind hand, I started to purr. For me, one performance particularly stood out. Helene, a Danish flautist whose workspace the loft was, brought in three other players to make up a flute quartet. My finest memory of that time was the group of us sitting around the quartet as they rehearsed a Mozart piece. Not only did the music fill the loft, it transformed it.

Amidst the beauty of the music we, as participants, got to observe the players. It wasn't actually a performance at all. Instead it was a rehearsal; they were practicing, trying stuff out. As a result, they stopped, questioned things and engaged with each other. How they related to each other, how they trusted each other and how they communicated fascinated us. We could see ourselves and our struggles through the work the musicians were doing. We could also ask ourselves how we fell short and how we could learn from what they did. What would it be like in an organisation if we supported each other like this, I wondered. As we continued to ask these questions we also got to try our own ideas out. We asked the players to turn their backs to each other and to try to play each other's parts. Through the music and the players, we got multiple perspectives; not only did we get our own perspectives, we also got that of the players. As a forum for human creative experimentation, it was boundless.

On the final day, we left the workshop for a tour of the recently completed Copenhagen Opera House where Helene played. On the way, I asked more questions and deepened my understanding. I could see metaphors in the music for the questions I had in my life and work. As we left the opera house I knew, although I had no idea how this would happen, this was something I wanted to explore further. It took some time, but a few years later I saw an opportunity and presented the idea to a client, who also loved it. As a result, I ended up taking Helene's musical experiment into a corporate setting where it had the effect of transforming a team's workplace and helping them to talk about all the issues they were having without any rational prompt. As I reflected, I realised how important it had been for me to be at that event. This, and many other things in my work over the years that followed, could be directly tracked back to that initially uncomfortable time of discovery and connection.

A series of experiences like Copenhagen have taught me how to deal with my own ongoing sense of 'imposter syndrome', a feeling that many of us have but rarely talk about. This is where we feel that we are in a place that is beyond us and that we will be found out. What we don't all realise is that surveys consistently show that 70-80% or more of us suffer from exactly the same thing. It is also something which only gets worse as we climb our life and career ladders towards ever more highly pressured expectations. In truth, when I ask a group to put up their hands if they suffer from it, very few hands, if any, stay down.

Events like this have helped because time has taught me that the feeling I have is simply a natural consequence of doing something new. My 'fear' tells me that I am growing into something new. There is of course risk in anything new, but like the musical opportunity, all the rewards lie here. The only way to escape the feeling is to stay entirely in my comfort zone, doing what I'm currently comfortable with. I have learned not to trust my love of comfort but rather my sense of beauty and my passion for the exciting. Now I take comfort from my discomfort and pair it up with my curiosity as a sign that I'm on to something exciting. The radical T-shirts with their cryptic references to music, art and philosophy I didn't yet know about may have made me feel uncomfortable, but the people wearing them didn't. Once I got to know them, they were a source of inspiration. What is more, going forward, I found that most of my best ideas sparked off a continuing stream of situations that stretched me just like this one had.

As well as not talking to our fears, we also rarely talk to each other about this feeling of inadequacy. In a world where everyone is suffering, we put on a brave face. Many times I have talked to one executive in an organisation who says something like 'Oh, it's all right for X, they are okay', when I know through working with X that that is simply not true. If anything, X is more senior and under even more pressure, with even fewer people to talk to about it. This is part of the problem: we think our sense of inadequacy will go away when we get to our destination. It doesn't. As we near the top, the solution to the problem that we might search for, the promotion that finally protects us, instead makes the situation worse. This is a good reason why we should get used to this feeling as early on in our lives as we can.

Once again, this is all very well, but the challenge is still that we do seem to stop our own progress. By chance I got talking to Lynne Parker, the founder of the women's comedy organisation Funny Women, about this at an event. I soon realised Lynne had a story to tell about how this capacity to block ourselves manifests in comedy. Initially, Lynne set up Funny Women as a challenge to the male-dominated comedy scene, and to address a contention she'd picked up on that women were not funny. As Lynne said, anyone watching a group of women talking who listens to the level of laughter between them will realise this is not the case. What Parker finds is that women use humour differently. Whereas men often use humour as part of their destination-driven agenda to tell a joke about something, women tend to use it to tell a multifaceted relational story.

Lynne and I agreed to meet up to investigate the subject further. When we did, Lynne's most striking statement to me was that women are more frightened of success than they are of failure. Curious, I asked her about this idea, and still remember her holding her coffee cup on a dark and cold afternoon, pausing to reflect on why she thought this might be. Lynne's considered answer was that women tended to have too many lines of thought going on. In Lynne's experience a man is more likely to accept success as a simple thing in his goal-based mindset, whereas a woman is more likely to see a multiplicity of issues surrounding her state and readiness for success. Whereas the man will just go for it, the woman can end up worrying about too many distracting things and get caught up in them, including things like how she might look and whether she has the right outfit. I would suggest that this isn't just a male/female thing but a spectrum in which many men of fertile imagination also worry about their own things. Our minds, our very own chattering Monkey and Beaver narratives, so easily stop us.

Although Lynne runs a comedy community and an annual Funny Women competition, much of her work centres around helping women who have no desire to be comedians to find their voice through stand-up. After all, if you can stand on a stage and crack jokes to an audience, what can't you do? In doing this she has found that the ability to nurture growth is what really makes the difference. What Lynne notices is that she has to work with the bit of the woman who wants to go on stage and do comedy. That part may not be visible right then but Lynne knows it is there because that individual has said that they want to give stand-up comedy a go at some point. The very fact that they are involved and talking about it in some way shows that they want to do it. It just comes to down to someone giving us the right bit of encouragement at the right time. 'Would you like to have a go next?' In response, the reluctant answer comes: 'Oh, all right…', and soon they are on stage, riding their fear and loving it.

What Lynne is doing is helping us to connect to a completely different form of power; a power that comes from within.

It is the same thing that we do as adults for children. Even if they are desperate to do something, really, they don't always feel like it in that moment. There is therefore a job to be done of providing a small amount of encouragement. It is the 'Why not give it another go?' after the third or fourth time of falling off the bicycle stripped of its stabilisers that leads to the breakthrough when they first ride those crucial few turns of the pedals without falling. It is the encouragement as well as the holding the bicycle and maybe even the little push we give as we release them fully to the wonderful moment when they realise they can do it.

At the same time, we have to be careful of the multiplicity of the mind that Lynne speaks of. Into a small nick of doubting, a branching series of cracks in thinking can appear. This can be something we do on our own, or it can result from a comment someone makes which we then amplify. A question such as 'Is that really a good idea at your age/in your state/position?' can be the single source of a whole train of negative thoughts about why this might not be such a great idea and what might go wrong. Imposed Power has a knack of cracking open our fears, and it's this that we want to move our energy and support away from.

This is why some of the most successful people around today surround themselves with positive people. Challenging people, talented people, and diverse people, but always positive people, interested in helping us to develop; this is an environment in which people can prosper on their own terms. In the safe, friendly green zone, we all get to be more relaxed. Here, we can grow through our challenges. Like a plant, we feel and find our way through.

In this supportive environment, reframing can really help us. It is not that the anxious feeling goes away but rather that we can change how we feel about it and how it weighs upon us. In particular, it is useful to know that the people who study such things can't tell us easily what the difference is physiologically between what we call 'anxiety' and what we call 'excitement'. Apparently, the chemicals released in the body and the processes that are stimulated by these emotions are physically much the same. This knowledge can help us to reframe how we interpret how we feel. That feeling in the pit of our stomach that we used to worry about, thinking it was our fear, we can now instead welcome as reassuring buzz of joy at the great thing that is about to happen. Now, we can almost worry if we don't have it, and when it does come, we can welcome it as a sign that something exciting is about to happen.

By making fear our friend we move beyond concepts of triumph or domination. This is no longer a competition, it is a cooperation. It's not that fear goes away, or that we defeat it. It is more like welcoming a stranger into our midst. Although we feel different with something new in the mix, life is now able to move on. Crucially, we are able to learn from the experience and to grow.

Now we know *how* we should do this, *what* are the clues we should be looking for that tell us what is calling us?

This question is where we go next.

What information do your fears have for you?

# 8. Anchoring Vertically

On a cold day, there is nothing like a fire to draw a crowd. As the little licks of yellow flame flicker, the glow of the hearth draws us in. Perhaps it's as close as we can get to the memory of the sun's heat on a hot summer's day. We can be reminded of that self-same light and heat, recovered in the frost of winter. Somewhere here there is a connection to our ancient cave-dwelling days as we seek comfort from the chills of the outside world, moving towards warmth. In the pull of the fire we come together, drawn towards an unspoken promise.

When Rob and I had agreed to do a retreat at this ancient Spanish farm in October he'd warned me that up here in the hills it would already be getting chilly. A walk outside in the day would still be pleasant, but the nights would be cold. Moving into November, the altitude made this old unheated place too frigid for anything, and I knew from a previous brief visit that by December the central fountain in the courtyard would be frozen up. Given this, the warming glow of a fire wasn't just desirable, it was a key part of the deal, a physical recognition that mankind's most enduring conversation always follows a consistent theme; a moving away from the wound we feel, towards some form of comfort.

An hour ago, in the late afternoon, I'd set the participants off on a task, and since then my main occupation had been to get the fire going. Some work holds a special pleasure for each of us. For me there is a special joy in the act of encouraging a fire. It starts with the first little flame, which then moves into a form that can sustain itself before it builds a body of heat, which can ignite ever bigger logs. Now the fire had established itself and the group was also now starting to come back together. In the courtyard, coffees were being made and conversations kindled over steam rising from hot drinks.

We were, however, missing one. Cath was not back. Initially, we decided there was no rush, and the consensus was to wait. A stirring of concern then slowly started to dawn. We rang a bell and I set out to find her. One participant suggested the pool, and that seemed a good place to check. I left the main courtyard through a large arched room cellared full of logs and walked down an avenue of trees towards the pool area to see what I could find.

The property we were lucky enough to be occupying is rich in history, having been purchased by the grandfather of my co-facilitator's wife, a successful local lawyer, after the Spanish Civil War. It is a *dehesa*, a farm built on marginal land that has always been difficult to make a living from, a challenge that requires some inventiveness, as the chief occupants of the land are holm oak trees and wild boar, together with a smattering of organically reared cattle. It is nevertheless a special place, farmed by the family today, where perhaps the same difficulty that results in the farm teetering on the edge of viability is also what gives it an inventive and engaging charm.

As I reached the top of a set of huge granite steps that led to the pool area I was relieved to see Cath propped up against a slab of stone, wrapped up in a blanket. She was intently looking in the direction of the pool, pencil and pad in hand. As I sat down beside her I could see why she had not responded, either to the hour or to the bell. Immediately I could see she was spaced out, in a world of her own, a world that had taken her someplace else entirely.

I wasn't sure if this was a good or a bad thing.

Cath had arrived early on the very first day and after a late lunch in a restaurant in the nearby town she'd told me about the juncture in her life that she had reached. For years she'd been a key player in a series of public projects that had grown ever larger, making both an increasing impact and her name. What I had no idea of were the personal struggles that she was facing to have got as far as she had. She'd now come to a crunch point which involved her leaving an organisation that had been very much her life – a decision that had tested her and tested her employer, who hadn't wanted to lose her any more than she really wanted to leave.

The theme for the retreat was 'Parenthesis', a bracketed time out for the participants to think about what was next in their lives. We'd spent the first day hearing what had brought each participant to this point and we were now starting to explore possible clues to their individual ways forward. The exercise we'd just started was an invitation for participants to spend an hour wandering in the environment around the house, led by their senses. The only instruction was to connect with something in which they found some beauty or fascination. There was no necessity for rationale in this, it was more a trusting to the environment that what they needed to find would show up.

The second half of the exercise was the process of unfolding what connected each person to the thing they found. In our discussion afterwards around the fire, these findings took us to places nobody had ever expected. As ever in these situations, the time we'd allocated was far from enough, but finally, just one participant was left. Cath took a breath and started to tell her tale. She first explained how she'd wandered around the grounds a bit lost, not really understanding the point of the whole thing. She'd even got to a stage where she'd given up. She told us how she'd decided to come back into the room with nothing, unable to show anything. This was the sort of feedback that made me extremely nervous. People giving up wasn't a thing I wanted. On the other hand, we were encouraging people to lose themselves and to let go. I realised that I had to stand back and let whatever happened happen; it all meant something.

With a few spare minutes of the hour yet to go, Cath explained that something had pulled her in the direction of the pool. She recalled that this was somewhere she'd actively avoided up to this point because it was a popular spot and a bit obvious. Now she approached the pool differently, freed from her previous desire to avoid the area. As she arrived she described how she was able to approach it afresh, as she sank down and relaxed into the utter beauty of the place. In particular, she'd started to look at the iron and stone structure which enclosed the rather green-tinged water. She then focused on the ornate granite structures which echoed the architecture of the house and surrounded the ancient spring water-fed pool. As she gave up to the peace she found herself in, her eyes had settled on a large spherical stone finial that sat on top of one of the granite posts. She'd then settled down with the blanket she was carrying and started to draw.

As she looked at this large object in order to draw it, she started to notice more and more about it. It was not just one colour. It was covered in lichens of various types which resembled islands holding their place on an earth-like globe where the seas alone remained a weathered granite grey. The huge finial, when one took the time to look at it, was full of minute life. It was also not a sphere. It may have looked like a geometrically defined object but even if it ever had been a sphere, it was no longer. It had hollows and imperfections, a life, a shape, a beauty all of its own. The beauty Cath was drawn to lay in those imperfections.

In that moment, Cath had shifted on her own axis. All her life, she explained, she'd only ever seen the sphere. She'd always sought to be what she felt she needed to be. In a world defined by spheres, anything that detracted from that quest to be what she thought she should be was an imperfection, a problem. Noticing the beauty in this massive piece of rock, Cath had found a different way of looking at herself. She didn't need to be anything else. She had everything she wanted already. She saw beauty in imperfection, her own and that of the world around her. It was seeing that beauty that had taken her someplace else entirely.

I could see tears forming in her eyes as the impact of this realisation set in. Much as she'd seen her truth already, speaking it in the room to others made it more real and brought out more emotion. Against a panel of regret for the past there was a leaping of joy for a future where a woman with a family at the peak of her career resolved that from now on she would cherish her own imperfections, the truth of who she really was and the unfolding possibility of her own creativity. She would, from now, prize what she had and who she could readily be over anything that she felt she ought to become. She didn't need to be anyone else's version of anything. By taking this step back into her own appreciation of who she was, she would naturally grow stronger based around a more solid core. This was an appreciation for herself and for the world around her, a deep engagement with what was really happening for her, that would change her entirely. I saw a woman truly radiating with an energy, brighter even than the fire.

Cath's breakthrough was life affirming for all of us, and it was a privilege to have been part of her experience. But much as it is a joy to be part of breakthroughs like these, I do increasingly question why this sort of self-knowledge has to be such a rarity, and why Cath had to go on the long track she did to find it. How is it that a tree finds it so easy to follow its true nature and to sense its way but that we, as more elevated forms of consciousness, can struggle?

Within our minds, there are essentially two different forms of self-awareness. There is, as we've seen, a capacity held by the Beaver to build and hold onto a narrative that both stretches back in time and projects forward. Within this form of self-awareness, we hold onto a story of who we think we are. I like to think of this as 'Horizontal' awareness in that it stretches out in both directions as far as we can see, providing plenty of space for us to get lost in. Here, our imagination can play games as it freely explores its largely unfettered ability to build its own worlds.

Directly contrasting with this is another form of awareness. This is the 'Vertical'. It is Vertical because it is firmly anchored in our sensory experience of the current moment. Here there is no story, no space to get lost in, simply an opportunity to engage more fully with what is with us now, filling our every sense with information. It is through this, more animalistic, rich Vertical awareness, that we connect with the world around us.

The problem is that most of the problems we have exist in the Horizontal rather than the Vertical. This is why mindfulness techniques focus on helping us to see the distinction and to notice the way the mind tends to constantly flit back into the Horizontal. It's difficult to stop this happening, and that is why we are normally encouraged to notice it happening and to bring the mind back to the present rather than to chastise ourselves for it. The problem is that we tend to spend an awful lot of time in our Horizontal awareness. Most of that time is at best wasted and at worst actually counterproductive. Fortunately, the solution is relatively straightforward, if a little difficult to actually achieve. It lies in a deeper exploration of the Vertical, together with a much more disciplined use of our imagination.

Just as in the previous chapter we started to ignore the Monkey by focusing on the Horse, I now want to introduce another animal to replace the busy story-making Beaver. This is the Dolphin. The Dolphin is a predatory mammal, but everything about dolphins speaks of acceptance, joy in the moment and letting go. Diving deep into the Vertical is the Dolphin's speciality. In *The Hitchhiker's Guide to the Galaxy*, Douglas Adams points out an essential misunderstanding between man and his water-loving friend. This is that man thinks he is more intelligent because he has achieved so much: New York, the wheel, wars and so on. Conversely, all dolphins have ever done is to muck about in the water having a good time. This, points out Adams, is precisely the same rationale for dolphins thinking that they are the more intelligent species.

Zoologists classify dolphins with whales and porpoises in the grouping 'cetacea', and this group's closest living relatives are hippos. This is because they evolved from a common ancestor that lived on land. Whenever I see a dolphin I think of an animal that knows it could have chosen to live on land but has decided not to. Dolphins are happiest where they are. There is something wise but supremely content about the Dolphin, and that is why it provides the essential remedy to the Beaver. Where the Beaver concentrates on the world just above and just below the surface of things, dolphins are creatures of depth. They are prepared to dive in deep, to seek out what is really going on. It is the curiously playful appreciation of Dolphin that is our theme here. This is exactly where Cath went.

Once again, the challenge tends to be not so much getting the idea of the Vertical and the Dolphin. Positive ideas like this are everywhere. The way forward is not so much the real issue here. The real challenge is understanding what it is that gets in our way and stops us from doing this, from engaging fully with the present moment.

One of the things I like to do is to enjoy the juxtaposition of being in the mountains or on the sea one day and in the thick of the corporate world the next. It's like the space we get when we return from holiday. It's a valuable time because briefly, as we sit in our normal lives with a bit of the holiday mind still in us, we see things that we normally wouldn't notice. In this delta, between two worlds, I find I see more clearly. I particularly like the contrast because it is an easy way of naturally being in the moment more, as we tend to be on holiday. One morning I was travelling into London when the challenge I was facing in order to stay present became more obvious. I'd just had a day off on the water and, feeling nicely balanced and open, I found myself noticing what was changing in me as I faced a busy day in the City of London. Ever since leaving home and our quiet country road to join the dual carriageway that morning I had been in a flow of commuter traffic. The flow started as I drove to the station, then continued as I parked and got on a train to London and kept going as I went underground to the Northern Line at King's Cross. Here the platforms are so full that waiting for the second or third train is the only real option on a busy weekday morning. All along I stayed with the flow, joining what seemed like the ever-increasing crush whilst watching its motions. As I got off the train at Bank, the flow at last peaked and then broke to some extent as people started to move in different directions. I went with the flow and came up to the surface, in the shadow of the Bank of England.

As I walked away from Bank towards London Bridge I noticed that more and more people were coming towards me. I'd gone so far south that I was now facing the main flow. I started to look at people and, in particular, at their faces. What I noticed straight away was that most people were looking down, absorbed in something. Some had headphones on, some were looking at their phones and others simply had their hands deep in their pockets. What surprised me more than anything was that I was so free to look at their faces as few even noticed that I was looking up and at them. What I realised, as I walked along looking around me, was not only how easy it was to get caught up in the flow, as I'd been, but also, once we are there, the trap it holds us in. More importantly, what struck me, as I looked at more and more distracted faces and hunched up bodies, closed into themselves, was that none of the people I was watching seemed to want to be where they were. Apart from the family of Chinese tourists I happened to see on London Bridge after my meeting who were the exact opposite, none of these people wanted to be here.

The picture of commuters walking north over Waterloo or London Bridge towards their jobs in the morning is a familiar image of the routine of work. What it masks is a bigger question of outcome and journey. When we get up in the morning our priority is to get to work. Given this waking desire to be somewhere else, how much of us wants to be where we really are at that moment? This is a distraction that it becomes easy to continue, because as soon as we get to work or wherever we need to be many of us will start thinking about where we'd rather be again. It might be lunch, it might be the gym, it might be home again or it might be a more distant thought, a holiday perhaps. All in all, it is easy to spend a great part of our lives not wanting to be where we are at all but rather wishing ourselves someplace else. We are in one situation, but at the same time find ourselves constantly imposing our alternative destination onto it.

What I realised as I stood on the street that morning was how outcome focused my life was and how easy it was to always be moving from the satisfaction of one outcome to another. As soon as one small challenge, like getting to a meeting, was achieved, another one – like getting what needed to be got out of the meeting – started. In a flash, I realised why sitting on the train could be so relaxing, as I literally let the train take the strain for once. If I could hand over the task of getting me to where I needed to go to the train driver, I could look out of the window and relax. Most of the time my life was focused on whatever my current desired outcomes were. These generally involved getting to somewhere else other than where I was. What I was doing was mortgaging the future as I effectively discounted the present in order to place all my bets on something shiny somewhere else. I could see not only how pervasive this strategy was but also how blind I was to it and how dangerous it was. It was all too easy to impose my desired future into my now and thereby completely lose any sense of presence.

I recalled a morning of bliss some years previously when, during a stressed and tired-out time, I'd gone out for drinks after work. It had gone on later than planned and, as usual, had been more than the one small drink I'd predicted. As a result, I'd ended up taking a later train and an expensive taxi home. Waking up in the morning a little worse for wear, I managed to structure my day to work from home, but one of my tasks was to rescue my car from the station car park. I felt I had no time to do so but decided my penance would be to cycle on my old small-wheeled folding bicycle to the station rather than getting another taxi or asking for a lift.

As I got my bike out my intention was to get the task done quickly so that I could get on with the day, in the spirit of obligation. The ride was likely to take me about three-quarters of an hour and with the drive back it was possible to be back in not much over an hour. However, as I set off, I changed my mind. I was still delicate, so I decided to dampen the motion of the constantly beating metronome that otherwise drove my life. I resolved to enjoy the cycle and decided to take it as slowly as I liked, taking in the scenery. As I went up the first hill, a rather large one, I simply took my time and enjoyed the gentle push on the pedals as I slowly made my way.

Across country, up the quiet lanes, into town I dawdled along, taking things as I pleased. I noticed the pheasants scared as I went by and I saw the gentle transitions from village to village and country into suburb. I started to look at the trees, see their different structures and to guess at their types. Before long I hit the busier roads and the bustling station and was almost surprised and a bit disappointed that my ride was over. I'd got to where I'd wanted to get, but what had happened was that I also felt a great deal better. I'd drunk a bottle of water on the way and my spirits had lifted. It was bliss. It may have been only a short cycle ride but it felt like I'd passed into a different way of living.

As I drove back home I realised that I'd held my destination lightly. I was conscious of the need to get to the station, but my focus was far more on the trip itself. If I'd met someone on the way I'd have been more than happy to stop to have a conversation. Taking time out for things that came up wasn't a problem; it was almost an invitation. I also noticed that I had no idea how long it had taken me and that it didn't really matter, partly because I'd got to where I was going quicker than I'd really wanted anyway. If I'd had to cycle home again I would even have accepted that too. I'd had a successful morning but not in the way I'd planned it. What was more, all the anxieties that had been weighing on me previously felt so much lighter.

It's not just the Dolphin that can help us here. Our friend the Horse also provides us with a perfect contrast to our own over-busy minds. A horse doesn't think ahead. It just gets on with it. If you are riding a long way on a horse, the horse doesn't ask how far it is to go, it just puts one hoof in front of the other, confident that it will get there.

The horse doesn't worry about how far it is or what might happen, it just gets on with the action now, which is all we can really do anyway.

'Make like a Horse' is therefore a simple and practical mantra to self; just be in that moment, take the next step and shut down any thought that is a thought as opposed to an observable reality. This is an ability to go Vertical in our awareness, allowing us to focus on the now and the fullness of what we are sensing now as opposed to anything else and to trust in our ability to cope. It works in a variety of situations including staving off all those bad and often somewhat depressing thoughts. If these thoughts are just a Horizontal flight of fancy, as opposed to a Vertical reality, are they really that much use? Is that problem we see really a problem right now? Whenever I feel the beginnings of depression I always ask myself where it is coming from. I have found that it always comes from crazy wanderings in the Horizontal. My response now is to shut those thoughts down and to relish the Vertical reality I see before me.

The cost of being human and having an agenda is that we customarily miss the beauty of the world around us. In our rush to get to the next thing we no longer stop to look at the beauty of the bud on the tree or to watch the bird as it flies high in the sky above us. If we stop and look all these things have an infinite beauty and intricacy about them. It is in this stopping to appreciate things as they are that we find love and joy. In this appreciation, we understand and make connection. When we stop to connect we see ourselves as part of an enabling system. When we truly see the beauty of the world around us we are at one and utterly complete.

The problem we face is that beauty and love have been completely hijacked by Monkey and Beaver. As early as Chapter 2, we finished with a cry to John Lennon's legacy of love as the answer, but it doesn't stand a chance whilst these two architects of Imposed Power tell us they are things to be attained or owned rather than something that simply exists. Beauty is simply the cry of the Vertical and love is our unadulterated appreciation for that Vertical experience. In its most simple terms, love doesn't mark the attainment of anything. It is quite the reverse. It is in the appreciation for things as they are and the desire for them to be the greatest they can be that love finds itself. There is no need in true love to change anything. Love is utterly unconditional. Love isn't anything… It just is. It is what we cherish with our pets, who love us and are glad to see us whatever. It is also why others often talk to our pets before they tackle us. The idea of externally imposed change is what corrodes any relationship. It is also the crack through which anxieties enter. Love is about unfettered appreciation. This is about the spending time to see the beauty of the rainbow rather than racing to the pot of gold that we think might be at its end.

The Christian mystic Thomas Merton once said, 'Do not depend on the hope of results… you may have to face the fact that your work will be apparently worthless and even achieve no results at all, or perhaps results opposite to what you expect. As you get used to this idea, you start more and more to concentrate not on the results, but on the value, the rightness, the truth of the work itself…'

Merton's warning is a good one, but the danger is, once again, that it has all the validity of a fusty old schoolteacher telling us to be flexible. We may agree with the sentiment, but that is not enough. We still have to ask ourselves why, in the lives we actually lead, as opposed to the ones we'd like to lead, we are so relentlessly pulled back into this goal-based, result-focused way of thinking. We know there is depth and truth in our work, and yet we are continually pulled away from its possibility by something that tells us that the achievement of an imposed destination is all that really matters.

As children, we probably asked our parents the question 'Are we there yet?' and, in a way, we are still asking that same question. Today we travel from one place to another in a continuing pattern that repeats itself over and over. As adults, we still travel in the same psychic space of goal expectation where once we journeyed expectantly to see Grandma. It's no longer an older family member that we are journeying towards but rather something else in the hierarchy, such as a meeting with the boss, a promotion or gaining a new client. In getting to our next goal there becomes a danger that our underlying need for outcomes themselves has become addictive. We stack them end to end in a continual ongoing flow where each stepping stone, once reached, leads to the next.

When I am out running I often remind myself of what I now call my 'Lack Hole'. I used to have a perfectly good pair of waterproof cross-country running shoes that got a bit old and started to leak. I put up with them for some time and even used to wear some Gore-Tex socks inside them to keep my feet dry on wet days. One day I started to convince myself that what I really needed was a new pair of running shoes. There may well have been an element of truth to this, as they were getting old, but the key thing was that I convinced myself that new shoes would transform my running. With the new shoes, I saw myself gliding sylphlike through the fields on runs longer and more challenging than any I had done before. I saw their glistening waterproof form as the solution not only to my wet feet but my conflicted soul itself. The shoes had a power beyond themselves and from that point, without something significant happening, it was just a matter of time before I made a purchase and realised my dream.

Eventually I put myself in the hands of a member of staff in an outdoor shop who genuinely climbed mountains and ran through wildernesses for fun. His expertise validated my dream, which was in turn suitably enhanced by not just a replacement of my old shoes but a better sole, a kinder fit, a finer liner and even a choice of colour. None of these things really mattered except in the way they enhanced the dream I had, in which my nirvana could be realised, the hole filled.

As I look down at the new shoes today, I see them as they are; shoes on my feet. Now muddy and with their own small scars, these shoes sit within the reality of my life in a way that the vision never had to. Just as the laptop I nearly bought was just a laptop and a shirt I bought was just a shirt. The laptop would have come with as many new problems as it solved whilst the shirt didn't inject any of the style I made it promise – it was just a shirt, as the shoes are just shoes. New boots can undoubtedly be a help, but my conclusion is that they are not the thing that I allowed the promise of them to become. I don't run in a more sylphlike way in them, nor do I run any further. Now I can see that the shoes are not the issue with my running. The real issue with my running is still my will to run – a more difficult issue entirely.

What I allowed the shoes to do was take on a greater meaning for me. They provided a solid container in which I could put my general sense of lack. The danger is that we all carry an underlying narrative that seeks the comfort represented by the fire; the warmth that solves everything. Again and again, that satisfaction can't be had and gets projected onto something more concrete. The mind would much rather find an external thing to be the solution rather than to have to question itself. What happens is that we see a series of destinations and things as the route to satisfaction. We are never 'here' because we are always focused on getting 'there', wherever that is. The problem is that 'there' is always somewhere else. This solution has a fault. It is temporary and never ending.

Just as we tell kids in the back of the car to keep quiet and enjoy the journey, we tell ourselves that we ought to do this too, but then promptly ignore our own advice as we focus on yet another destination. And this perennial focus on outcome, whatever situation we apply it to, whether it's a conversation or a life, lies at the heart of Imposed Power. It's having an outcome-driven agenda that gives us a reason to impose – on others, and also on ourselves.

Now, having observed it over the years, I see my 'Lack Hole' as something that will always be there to some extent. A hole arises because there is something missing in the whole. As John Stewart Collis observed, at the birth of consciousness we separated ourselves from nature. That separation created a feeling of something being missing, and that feeling is still there. We feel disconnected and our fear tends to reinforce this feeling. Indeed, fear is used as a tool to divide us and promote more separation. This means that once again it is the mind that both created the lack in the first place and which now tries to fill it for us. Given this complicity, it's not surprising that it might not want us to notice what it has done.

This push towards something that will complete us combines with our comprehensive ability to imagine what the future might be like. In one sense reality doesn't stand a chance as our visions of what the holiday could be like take over. When we finally get there, it is never quite as we imagined. In the same way that our fears multiply in our imaginations, so do our pleasures. This is perhaps why books, fiction in particular, are so attractive to us as we lose ourselves in their worlds, unfettered as they are by reality.

What I have learned is the lesson of the shoes: to never expect the Lack Hole to be filled by anything, and to double check my fertile imagination. This is where the Dolphin comes in, with the realisation that it's only by being able to muck around in the water and have a good time that the feeling of needing to get somewhere else goes away. The mind, with its Horizontal projection and its relentless promise of it all being better if only x, y or z would happen, is the root cause of the problem.

Anxiety exists in the gap between what we have and what we'd like to have. If that gap persists and continually needs filling, our anxiety will be greater as a result. If we allow ourselves to be victims of this feeling rather than masters of it, we will always struggle to master our fears. If, on the other hand, we realise we are already complete, the pressure value will fall a notch. It's by a Vertical appreciation of what we have, in ourselves, in the world and in the people around us, that we regain a stabilising anchor and, at the same time, see the truth that is already there to be found.

It is our sense of beauty that leads us to the things that matter to us the most. It also connects us to the truths about ourselves that we struggle to explain logically. Language – the labels we give things – can be a hindrance in this regard. One of my own breakthroughs in this area came through a technique called 'focusing', invented by Eugene Gendlin. Born in Vienna, Gendlin and his family moved first to Holland to escape the Nazis and then on to America. He grew up being fluent in many different languages and was familiar with the limitations of language and his own ability to name feelings accurately. Gendlin was more trusting of the body's ability to lead us to the answers. He saw it as more than a physical thing. He saw our body as a sensor, a sensor that was also part of a bigger system.

Focusing is a technique in which we build a 'felt sense' in our connected and sensing bodies about our observations and the things that trigger them. Rather than just naming or immediately trying to use what we already know to label this felt sense, Gendlin encourages us to spend time with the feeling, to locate it and to feel its quality. Eventually we get a 'handle' for the felt sense; a word that fits to it. We then alternate between the word and the felt sense to check the fit, changing the word perhaps more than once, if, as often happens, it is not quite right. We do this until we feel we have resonance between the two.

The real power of focusing is that it leads not only to more feeling but also potential breakthroughs in what *fuels* that feeling. It does this by moving from the feeling itself into a phase of asking about our needs. We ask in this stage why the feeling is there as we build a bridge between our needs and the feelings that for many of us have been eroded by logic and what we are told by others. Instead of the ready answer we might have, we question what our real unmet need is. We stay with this until we get a shift, a realisation of something we didn't previously know. This shift is generally about why that feeling is there and what it perhaps was previously failing to tell us. What surfaces is a need we weren't conscious of before. We finish by acknowledging the shift and recognising the pathway that we have just opened up.

The first time I tried focusing, I used it to give me an answer about some issues I was having at work. Years before, I had a new US boss and one of the new things he insisted on was approving all my travel, including the cost and timings. I was getting really annoyed with the situation and with him. I had to fly to the US for a client presentation and he kept mentioning that he regularly flew economy. This wasn't something I did on business, particularly back overnight from the States, when I tended to work the next day. I was getting more and more anxious. I had assumed that this was all about cost cutting and it felt a bit personal, as if my job was also under threat. What I realised when I tried focusing was that this wasn't about him or the flights at all. The feeling I got when I isolated it was all about my own autonomy. I saw that I needed more freedom in my work. This realisation eventually led to my changing jobs. More immediately, as soon as I relaxed, I stopped being anxious. I then got his approval for the flights without any problem. I saw how easy it was to completely misunderstand my own feelings and thereby fall into an unhelpful way of solving them.

This wasn't all I saw, however. As I look back on this time now, I see how my reading of the situation had also allowed me to fall into Monkey's original trap. It was just too easy to be a suffering Monkey and make my new boss the villain. Blaming him had made me instantly feel better. All I'd really done was to give myself victim status. It was almost as if the certainty of that role and the clarity that gave me mattered more than my seeing a better way forward. In truth, the oddly satisfying rush of pleasure I felt as a victim was just an easy way to avoid facing up to my real challenge.

Dolphins don't have these problems of misunderstanding. They echolocate by sonar, relying less on vision than we do, and this means of connection gives them distinct advantages. Experimental film director David Cronenberg once talked about this in a magazine interview when questioned on his treatment of taboo. Whereas we repress what comes from the inside, including our less desirable excretions, dolphins are more open. They don't suffer from the same need to create a secondary narrative. Cronenberg's point was that, by using sonar, dolphins read each other's emotions directly. Because one dolphin gets to read the configuration of the viscera of the other it can tell whether the dolphin it is meeting is tense, happy or sad. Part of the dolphin's toolbox is to be innately connected with what is going on inside. This is a key part of the Dolphin's magic; they don't just read what is going on inside themselves, they can also read what is going on inside other dolphins. Do we still think we are smarter than dolphins?


I didn't realise the extent of my own complacency until I nearly lost my sight in one eye. One night I was walking back to King's Cross Station in London when I noticed that half my vision out of my right eye had gone. I had no idea when this had happened, what had happened or how. I went to bed that night confused and when I woke up it was still there, or rather not there. Later that day I went to my own doctor, then a local eye specialist, and from there was admitted to Moorfields Eye Hospital to have surgery on what turned out to be a detached retina.

In the clinic waiting for surgery I got speaking to Richard, a boy in his late teens who was with his parents, up from Wales, a day's travel from his remote rural home. I learned that as a child his eyesight had never properly formed in either eye and that he'd gone on to totally lose his sight in one eye. The hospital had managed to give him a thin murky view from the other eye and it was through this that he now saw what he could. Richard's life was heavily curtailed by his limited sight and he was highly dependent on his parents, both of whom were with him.

As we spoke, I began to understand the effect that Richard's eyesight problems had on his life. Here was someone who'd never been able to take anything to do with his sight for granted as I had. This was through no choice or action of his own, but it affected everything in his life and that of his family. As he spoke I realised why he was here. He risked now being told that he was finally losing the small amount of sight that he did have. All his life he had known that he was clinging on to the limited amount he had by a thin thread and now there was a chance that he'd be told that this delicate link would itself be cut in the near future.

It was only as Richard described to me the limits of what he saw that I started to understand that I'd never really be able to see what his life was really like. In what for me was a clear and brightly lit room of people, I struggled to imagine what it was like to only be able to see through a narrow field of vision in one cloudy eye. This was partly because Richard had no experience of what I could see either. Whilst this conversation with Richard was totally different from a conversation I might have had with someone at work the day before, at the same time it was identical. I realised that I could never see things as any other person did, and any idea that I could was naïve at best. Why would I ever seek to impose my perspective, my fear, my strategy, on anyone else?

At the time, I was dealing with the challenges of a new leadership role. I had to find answers to a series of problems including how to bring two separate functions that I was responsible for together. My experience with Richard gave me the answer. I saw that I was it was okay not to know. I saw that my own perspective was limited anyway. It felt uncomfortable, but the thing I had to do was to listen to everyone. I had a feeling that if I did this the answer would come. It was out there; I just had to open myself to it instead of sitting alone racking my limited brain to find an answer. My fear and my desire to rush to an answer had been stopping me from doing what I most needed to do.

As a result, I sat down with every member of my team and listened to what they had to say. It took a month, but it gave me the answers I needed. It also changed the way I led and communicated forever. Once I opened to it, I saw the richness of the network that had been there all along. At the same time, I was humbled by how relatively little I knew. Fortunately, my fears of being found out never materialised. Strangely, no one else seemed to realise what I feared. I could now see that the fear I felt was my own invention. I saw that I could let go of what had been driving me, appreciate what was there and lead all at the same time, if only I was prepared to let go of my fear in the first place.

The ability to let go is a central tool in our approach. One of the reasons I know this is because I once got the chance to ask a room full of wise minds the answer. In a leadership session with a selection of primary school children I asked them to show me, on a count of 1-2-3, how they would physically represent power. As the count of three settled in the air, I looked at a room of children frozen in different shapes and was stumped. I had half expected prowling figures or some claws, but what I saw was a huge variation with no consistent pattern. In my moment of confusion, I was lost, seized by what I thought I might see. Fortunately, I remembered to ask the children to tell me about their shapes. One after another they rushed to explain their tightened fists, their solid poses and their arms held high. Then one young boy gave the answer which brought it all together. 'I'm all tensed up,' he said.

Suddenly a consistent theme became clear. Everyone was tightened up, in fists, in arms, in muscle, in jaw. Power was represented by a tension, held physically in the room. We were each holding on to a stance, locking ourselves down in a way of being. We displayed our power by locking up, pumping ourselves full. I find this same thing with adults when we ask them to put themselves in a fear situation. The shapes are different but what is consistent is this locking up, this tensing of the body. In these fear positions, we dis-ease ourselves. Power and fear share this and the only way to change and move forward is to recover the flow and to let go.

Our friend the Dolphin is constantly letting go. We overestimate the importance of holding onto our own ideas and beliefs just as we overestimate the importance of the in-breath; the in-spiration. In all this holding on, there is a danger of seizing up, of loss of flow, of forgetting to breathe out. It is in this letting go of what we have that we find the space to take in what is truly there and to be warmed by it.

In Chapter 7 we learned to make fear our friend. By holding what we fear closer, we begin to see what our challenges are and how to address them. Here, in Chapter 8, as opposed to being anxiously caught up in what might be, we've seen how we can build a deeper appreciation. It is through connecting Vertically to what is here, that we anchor to what is.

The question now is how we bring these strands together. It is this weaving weft that we look at next. How can we bring what we've learned about growth, challenge and appreciation together to build a new model for how we see our fears through a different lens of power?

What stops you noticing what is already there for you?

# 9. Enabled Power

The next question Alex asked me was the most difficult I'd faced so far.

'What do you want me to carve on the tree?' he asked. Having set the hare running, he then immediately took the pressure off. 'It's all right, I don't need an answer right now, next week will do just fine,' he added with a grin.

I had known this moment was coming for some time, but until now naming the tree and saying something about it had just been an occasional fluttering visitor in my imagination. Now, it was something real and expected. I could see that Alex was curious as well as workmanlike. Finally, I had to make a choice about what this was all about. I now felt the growing pressure of what I chose to say about this project. It was about to become both public and permanent.

The idea had come out one of many discussions I'd had over the years with the headteacher of our village primary school. This particular branch of engagement was about how we, as a family, whose two children had now passed through the school, might mark this passing out. We wanted to give the school something meaningful, of lasting value. My wife and I had talked about this on and off for months but had failed to settle on anything in particular. None of our ideas – a bench or some play equipment perhaps – was particular enough to us. We knew there was a better idea but it had taken a while to reveal itself.

The head's office was somewhere I got used to for all the wrong reasons in my days of school. It was somewhere that I knew I didn't want to be. It was there – and maybe even on the way there – that I tended to learn things about myself that I didn't want to hear. I'd be scared before I even got there. A state of high defence is never a good time to hear what is said. The whole body is ready for the attack, prepared for fight or flight. We know that we don't want to be there. Who really wanted to be in the head's office or, even worse, waiting outside, if they could avoid it? This time, fortunately, was different.

'You know,' the head said as she calmly considered my question,

'We have a bunch of prizes for sporting achievement, but we have nothing for what this school is really known for, for looking after others, for community spirit.' From her perspective, she went on to say, this was something that knitted with how she saw us as a family. I hadn't really thought about it, but she was right. This observation did capture both my wife's and my own lack of ability to win anything on the sporting field, a tradition now picked up by our children. I also recognised in it a far greater truth I hadn't seen quite so clearly until then. The need to compete and to beat others had never been who I *really* was. As a family, we thought about different things from sport and winning. Suddenly, the answer to our question became a whole lot clearer. I went away from the meeting wondering why I hadn't had this conversation earlier.

The tree grew from this small grain of an idea. By chance I was already talking with Alex, the son of friends in the next village who had himself been a pupil at the school. Alex was busy pursuing a career in sales but he also nurtured a fertile design business where he was building a range of eclectic objects in wood. I loved what he was doing and wanted to commission something from him. The only problem I had, given how prolific he was, was deciding what it would be. Suddenly, these two meandering streams came together and made one strong river. Alex would make us something in wood to capture the idea of community spirit. Before long it became clear what it would be. Our wooden object would take the form of a tree.

Every year now my family now gets to go back to school for the annual prizegiving at the end of the summer term. The feeling I get from being at a primary school, with the unbridled energy and noise of a group of small children on a summer's day, is perhaps one of my favourite feelings in the world. This is partly what now makes this prizegiving a particular favourite. We get to present our slightly unusual community award and to explain the origins of what is now 'The Friendship Tree' to the children who might be new to it.

The seed for the idea was actually planted during an earlier conversation I had with the head some years before. I'd decided I wanted to do something for the school using my mediation skills, and in order to finally see if I could make something happen I'd booked an appoint-

.ment to see her one afternoon. This was no ordinary meeting, peppered as it was with interruptions from the myriad people who needed this critical person's immediate attention. I had, however, come at a good time, as the school was preparing for anti-bullying week.

The head told me a story about bullying. When she first arrived, she asked everyone she could if there might be any at this delightful village school. 'No,' she was told, 'Not here.' Whilst happy with that answer, she then asked a different question. She asked the kids, 'If there was any bullying, where would it happen?' Immediately she got an answer. She was consistently told that if it did happen it would take place in a quiet, out-of-the-way spot at the back between two classrooms. 'Aha,' she thought. What concerned her was that she could now see that bullying not only happened, as it does in many places, but that it also had a place.

Although I went into the meeting with no clear answer to what I could do to help, I came out with more than enough to be getting on with. The first action was for me to take a class during anti-bullying week in which I talked to the kids about bullying and how we might think differently about it. The idea of entertaining and engaging a class of small children terrified me, and as a result I spent a lot of time preparing a talk and a plan. I'd have saved a lot of time and effort if I'd just done from the start what I ultimately ended up doing: provoking and talking to them and then reacting to what they had to say, rather than sticking to the elaborate plan I made. Still, plans help us to be calmer than we would be and to have a fallback, which is their real value in my experience. Plans can be a trap; it's the preparation we get by a bit of planning that is essential.

The class went well, but more importantly it spawned a smaller group of the elder kids in the school who were interested in doing more. I met up with this group subsequently after school, and as I spoke to them I realised my interest was driving the conversation in a particular direction. Although I had a lean towards resolving conflict and mediation, their interest was much more about how they built positive relationships from the start. I realised that if I followed what I was finding here, rather than what I wanted to impose, the outcome would be different. I decided to go with what I found.

What they liked was the idea of what they referred to as 'BFF' – Best Friends Forever. This idea also became the basis of the group's name: 'Friendship Finders'. In one of our discussions I took this theme and built on the head's realisation that bullying had a place. I asked the children about where they felt our efforts to help kids who were struggling should locate itself in the school. We walked around the grounds thinking about this until the children settled on a large tree with a seat around it at the back of the playing field. This tree became base camp for the Friendship Finders, and in time became somewhere a child in need could go for help.

Alex's tree extended these ideas into something new. The finished Friendship Tree that he created effectively builds on the original one in the playground. It is made from several layers of wood and now sits on the wall in the entrance hall to the school. It is the best part of a metre high, twice that wide and not much thicker than a finger. The greatest thing perhaps is that it is not just a model of a tree. I got talking to a young local blacksmith who sells his wares at the school's Saturday market and we came up with the idea of adding fruit and leaves which he provides. Each year the child or children who are selected for the award get a cast metal apple which is put on the tree with their name and the year. In addition, each child gets to take away a small metal leaf key ring. Over the years that have passed, the tree bears fruit and, I hope, the keys carried on those rings unlock more doors. The award is made to a child who the head and teachers feel has gone out of their way to help others during the year.

In answer to Alex's question, I also had an idea for some words for the tree that had been floating around in my head for some time. These were inspired by a poem written by Dawna Markova on the night her father died. In 'I Will Not Die An Unlived Life' Markova gives herself the challenge of opening up to living more fully. It's a powerful piece in which she talks of her preparedness to embrace her fears. She ends the poem with the model for living she wants to adopt. This is to live so that what came to her as seed develops into blossom and what came to her as blossom goes on as fruit. I went for some time turning over this idea in my head as I thought about the tree. This core idea of being a part of a responsible and nurturing system of growth captured perfectly what we were doing. With apologies to the original beauty of the poem, Markova's inspiring words and imagery became in my head the thought 'Let that which came to us as seed go on as fruit'. It was these words that we put on the tree.

This image of seed to fruit captures the essence of how the alternative system of power I want to share with you works. The seed says to us that we already have the essential components that we need in most situations that we face. It is not that we don't need anything, for a seed surely needs certain basic things such as light, water and air to prosper. Ultimately, the seed exists as part of a system. What the seed doesn't need, however, is to wait for someone else to arrive to do the building work, to tell it where the light is coming from and to direct what should be done. There is no need to impose a structure on the seed, for it has the essentials already, by the very fact of being a seed.

I call this form of power 'Enabled Power'. Enabled Power is the power we all have through the very act of living. It is our power, driven from a sense of who we truly are and want to be, to make choices and decide for ourselves. Imposed Power, which is external to us, comes from above us, with a sharp, aggressive and perhaps mechanical imposition upon us. Enabled Power comes from the other direction entirely. It comes from within us and harnesses our innate strengths. Like a plant or the trees we looked at in Chapter 6, it seeks the light. Enabled Power looks for space to grow and sees opportunity. As it grows, it builds its own rooted system that sustains and connects it. Enabled Power anchors and grounds itself, as it grows upwards.

Here we find a fundamentally different approach to the themes of fighting, competition or dominance proposed by Monkey. It is what we find in the safe green zone of the traffic light. This form of power is no longer a battle, and to embrace it we need to be aware of the old stories we hold as well as building a new one. Crucially, this requires us to see the prevailing narrative of the 'Monster Story'; the idea that everything worthwhile comes out of conquest over an enemy. This is a narrative structure we see in many of our favourite stories and movies. It drives the plot line of every James Bond movie, most Hollywood disaster and action movies and the core conflict at the heart of the *Star Wars* films. The idea of a battle of good over evil is one we so easily translate into our lives. If we continue to believe this default story, and to copy it, we stay with Imposed Power, in a war with the oppressor.

Instead, Enabled Power takes on another narrative we already know. It is that of the love story. All the best love stories are made up of a heady mixture of desire and appreciation, coupled with challenge. In attitude, it is as different from how oppressed we might feel on the worst day of winter to our joy on the most fertile day of summer. There are still challenges, but they are different in the warmth. Any love that is captured too easily doesn't make a great story, and so it is here. The greatest growth comes from the bigger challenges and the biggest challenges come from the greatest love.

This is not some simple story of love conquering fear however. As we've seen, our fears are complex and rich in information. In the film *Donnie Darko* there is a scene where the main character Donnie and his class at school are forced to sit through some training promoted by fear guru Jim Cunningham. The guru's methodology, illustrated on a simple scale, is that we should choose love, in the positive energy spectrum, rather than fear, in the negative. This might sound compelling, but when Donnie is forced to consider an example involving a lost wallet, then to go up to the blackboard to put a cross on one end or the other of the spectrum to capture it in terms of fear or love, he refuses to.

Donnie then argues to his evangelical teacher that neither the example nor life are that simple. He's right because, as he's seen in what he is facing, there is no simple way of dividing things up. As Donnie says in his frustration, we have to take account of the whole spectrum of human emotion. We can't just deny our fears and choose love. If we did, we'd lose a rich source of valuable clues to what we need to investigate next. What we have is a rich texture in which the positive and negative are in a mix. Indeed, there is no way of ever judging anything as definitively good or bad anyway. And, as we've seen, the 'negative', our fears, holds all the information for us anyway. The only way through, as Donnie finds out, is by a loving acceptance of your fears in their rich entirety, wherever that takes you.

This is the way in which two seeming contradictory threads, fear and love, the themes of the previous two chapters, come together. It is in this intertwining of appreciation and challenge represented by our Dolphin and Horse guides that Enabled Power thrives. What starts as a tender growth grows into a structure as strong as a great tree. This doesn't happen because it is easy; it happens because we have a strength of desire that we are consistently challenged to fulfil. The challenge and the meeting of that challenge mutually reinforce each other. Like a child learning to walk, it is the strengthening that comes through the falling that gives us the muscle and balance we need.

The seed's first difficulty is that on its own a seed might be said to look like any other. There is nothing external to show the seed's promise. Jack had to be convinced that the seeds that grew into the magic beanstalk had this potential within them. His mother, perhaps more rationally, could not see anything until they had grown in the morning. In this doubting lies a truth. It can be difficult to appreciate the potential that lies within. Part of the reason for this is that the seed is not a solitary thing. The seed finds itself in a situation. That placing, in arid, rocky or fertile ground, affects it. Then, as it grows, the conditions it meets and how it reacts to them will change the course of its life. It is not that the external world doesn't matter. It matters a lot. It is just that the seed's relationship with the external is different. It doesn't look to the world to solve everything for it. Instead, it accepts and uses the conditions it finds.

It is in the process of growing that we find out most about ourselves. I used to think that the creature that best captured change and breakthrough was the caterpillar as it settles down to pupate into a butterfly. I thought that what was important was the caterpillar's preparedness to stop. As I saw it, the stopping was necessary to allow things to gestate. I've now realised that although a breakthrough might happen this way, none of my changes themselves have come through quiet introspection. They have come through taking action, action on the field that's real and visible to other people. It is in the interaction and connection with the world from which the biggest opportunities for growth come. We do need to reflect, but it is in the doing, the experimenting and being open to wiping the slate clean, rewriting our stories at the fundamental level, that the breakthroughs lie.

Growth can be a chicken-and-egg question, in that often we get stuck, not knowing what to explore until we explore it. Fortunately, the seed has an answer. The first sign of life from a seed is that of the initial taproot, a strong initial root that emerges through the skin of the seed into the ground. This root is what establishes the growing plant and is its first definition. Just like the seed, we each have a similar taproot that is ready to define us. As well our visible growth, we also have this central root which is our sense of purpose and commitment. This root develops with us. We grow though continual challenge, but at the same time, we are also rooted.

Our taproot is our central stabilising force. Clues to it might lie in our ancestry, ideas passed on to us from our parents or grandparents, or it might be a challenge that lies unsolved for us in our past. The things that upset us can also give us an insight into it. We may see this root in the passions and interests of our own childhood, before bigger ideas took over. Alternatively, we might see it in our future. We all have a passion that drives us and ultimately defines us. Sometimes it lies deep, for it is connected to our soul.

Often, we struggle to connect this sense of who we are with the jobs that the world offers us. This is a problem with the Imposed Power approach that seeks to squeeze us into a space that already exists. It's a world where the careers office is full of brochures but none of them are really us. We may well not fit for good reasons. Many of us feel this mismatch – between who we really are and what we feel pressure to be. One day we might even realise that we are doing a job we don't actually like. Perhaps the job we do is just the one we pushed ourselves into or perhaps fell into. We feel stretched; the gap between the root of who we are and what we are expected to be feels too large to bridge.

By having a strong sense of what our root is, everything we need to do becomes clearer. Once we are rooted, with a sense of purpose, even our deepest fears seem less significant. Because we are committed to something big our fears, in turn, take on a different, smaller, role. We now have a reason to take on a challenge. We know now that we are doing this for a reason. Our bigger, more relational, more eternally sourced driver adds something to our energy for growth. Fear pales in the presence of true commitment.

Ten years ago, I might have denied the idea that I had such a root. The careers office at school started a process that told me I had to go into the world and become a thing that already existed, to take a job, a role, to simply choose what others told me. The world of Imposed Power existed for me to find my way into and fit in where I could. No one said that I should take time to examine who I was and what I wanted to achieve. The process I went through when I started to know I needed to leave my job was what helped me finally to find my taproot. I don't even know if I fully understand it now, but what I do know is that I am getting closer. My taproot is an internal thing that only I can truly feel. It needs the world to stimulate it, but it's only my sensory connection to it that tells me in precisely what direction I want to explore. Once I find this, it is easy to commit.

It is in the testing it out that we learn most. My first take was that I was driven by helping people to work better together. To this end I pursued mediation and conflict resolution. After a while I could see that although this was a skill I had, it wasn't what really drove me. I only found this by testing my original hypothesis in practice and watching how it played out for me, not in the world of my mind but in the external world.

An example of this learning came when a client suggested I help two individuals who weren't getting on to resolve their differences. I met with both and realised that one of them simply wasn't prepared to compromise or change. In my report back, I told my client that my chances of success were low and that I'd rather not mediate. At the time, I struggled to fully understand why I had turned away work of the type I allegedly sought. I did, however, suggest that I'd be happy to work with the other person, the more junior of the pair, to help him deal with the other and to grow as a leader. In one way of thinking, I was fearful that I'd just walked away from an easy piece of work. Six months or so later, though, my original offer got accepted. Years have now passed and my new client has now taken over from his nemesis and is flourishing. I learned through this, and a series of experiences like it, that my taproot wanted to grow in a different direction than simply resolving conflicts. It is more about helping people grow to their full potential than it was about sorting out differences. It is often only through this type of practical exploration of what our roots are that we get to fully understand our own drivers.

What the seed doesn't have to do is to wait for the external world to give it instructions. It has the resources it needs to get going. The power it has is 'enabled' because of this balance between the internal and the external. We are all 'able' because the root of this power lies with us, at our core. At the same time, there is an enabling element that is systemic and lies outside us. We all need a bit of help from time to time, partly because everyone's ability has its limits. This might be the provision of some fertile soil for the first growth, or it might be the nudge given by a caring friend. It is the friendly prompt that Lynne knows she has to give occasionally to get someone on the stage and off. Ultimately, we have a mutual dependence on each other, because life is relational.

How we help each other is critical. This means a supportive positive environment. When it is needed, we can be challenging to others, but when we do this we are helping them to define their own challenges rather than imposing anything on them. We might ask, 'What are you going to commit to do?' In time, we can reinforce the structures and challenges they themselves have committed to. In this, we are not telling anyone what to do. We are instead asking them how they are doing against the challenge they have set themselves. What we are doing is to helping a person who is already fundamentally able to build and maintain their own path of growth.

Our growth is also highly dependent on our finding alignment between it and our strengths. Strength is a much-misunderstood idea, however. Unlike a muscle, which strengthens as we use it, these strengths tend to be more innate to who we are. Being good at something doesn't mean it is an innate strength. When I was a lawyer, I used to think that detail was a strength of mine, and indeed it seemed to be. The problem was that after a day in the detail I was exhausted. This wasn't really a strength of mine – it was simply something I had become good at. In fact, the more I did the detail the more I disliked it. I could feel a rebellion growing, but at the time I didn't understand the feeling. Now I know detail is not my strength and, what is more, now I am free of my old story, I can see that I positively avoid it.

Our true strengths are the things about which we have genuine passion. We have good days and bad days. Our real strengths are often the things that we have been doing when we have a great day. If we have been busy all day, perhaps caught in the flow of what we are doing, yet emerge with a sense of energy, the likelihood is that we are playing to our strengths. If we have spent a day doing what we know, but emerge low on energy, then it is not our strength that we are playing to but merely our learned behaviour. A truly draining day is often a clue that we are heading in a direction that is not truly us.

Having a true strength can be the opposite of being good at something. Competency is no guide and overuse can be what finishes us off. We will eventually tire of what we don't really love, however good we are at it. Conversely, if we have a passion for something, it doesn't really matter that we struggle with it. If we have passion we will quickly get better. If we love the guitar we won't mind the sore fingers, but if we hate it we will think of nothing else. We should follow the passion more than the ability, for the ability will follow the passion soon enough.

Passion is also something we have to temper. Our sensitivity is double edged since our tender, early shoots of growth are both highly appreciative and potentially highly reactive. We have to get used to life's equivalent of the head's office. If we are to learn we have to keep calm and to listen to what we are told. Our attitude to what we sense is often what makes the critical difference. We either take in what we sense and respond to it creatively, or we react to it badly. This can even be put in an equation:

$$P = C \times A^2$$

where performance (P) relates not just to the 'C' of competency but also to the 'A' of attitude in a multiplying factor where the 'A' is at very least squared. This is about an attitude of making the most of everything. It is about riding our fears.

This is what eventually happened at the bomb scare Fear Hack. It is in this giving up to what *is* that we find our answers. When Russian chemist Dmitri Mendeleev managed to arrange the chemical elements by atomic number and their recurring chemical properties into the genius idea that is the periodic table, he did the final task in his sleep. It was only by letting go of all that he held so dear in his ordered waking mind that he was able to seize what was really awaiting, ready to be found. This ability, of being able to see the emergent but as yet unknown way in which the differences we have can be integrated into a single unifying system, is the process of life.

The problem here is that we have all been born in a period where Imposed Power has long become normalised. We have also fallen victim to Thomas Hobbes' 17th-century idea that life in a state of nature is 'solitary, poore, nasty, brutish and short', and thus to be avoided at all costs. This means the fruits of Enabled Power and the possibility that we might feel connected, rich, kind, caring and joyful instead, feel out of sight. We expect the solution to an empty piece of land to be development, not growth. We have a power model that increasingly focuses on money at the cost of everything truly valuable to us as humans. We approach land as 'real estate' for exploitation rather than the natural sustaining wilderness it really is. We don't see that we are part of a connected whole, that we depend on plants, insects and birds and the whole of the natural system around us as much as anything. We then carry this necessity for imposition through into our lives.

At the extremes, many of us suffer from a feeling that someone else, not us, controls our lives. This is the fastest recipe for depression that anyone could prescribe. We feel down quickly and then stay there because we feel we are no longer free to make decisions for ourselves. This robs us of a vitality that is a fundamental human need. The antidote is not to take drugs. It is a realisation that there is an alternative to Imposed Power and that we all have a genuine opportunity to take back control of our lives in balance with others. We do not have to put up with this abuse of human potential. We could choose to move away from measures of monetary and economic growth that are external to us and instead move towards behaviour that promotes our collective internal growth.

Much as we might see the troubles in the world and the abuses of power around us, this is not something we need to fix in other's lives. The truth is that we have to tackle it ourselves first. It is from here that Enabled Power starts. We have to face up to the fact that our problem is largely self-made. In order to be able to grow as we wish to, we have to stop getting in the way of our own growth. Interference is something we humans do very well. Life in the wild doesn't get in its own way. We not only domesticate animals, we domesticate ourselves. This domestication necessarily involves submission. We get used to it as we grow up, then we adopt it for ourselves and teach it to our own children. This the normalisation of a model where we have got so used to imposing solutions that we no longer see it.

To get out of the way of our own growth, we have to let go of what we may habitually want to impose on the situation and let the appreciation of Dolphin in. It shouldn't need the flashing blue lights of a police car or being fired from our jobs to wake us up. I now accept that I could have been far more alive to the unease I felt in the lift coming into work. I avoided it at the time, but if I'd let go of my suppression of it I'd have learned far more from it. It was trying to tell me to be more human, and being human involves pain as well as pleasure. Where we feel discomfort, we have to learn to accept it in order to learn from it. There will be a release eventually if we allow that pain to be. Accepting its full flow will be difficult, but it is by doing so that we will hear what it has to tell us. In being heard it will tell us more, allowing the emotion that fuels it to fully surface. Most importantly, it is by allowing ourselves to fully feel the pain that we build a reservoir of commitment to change. That commitment is the root of our growth.

This commitment is something we have to hold lightly. As we have seen, if we attach too solidly to a particular outcome we drift into imposition ourselves. Goals can drive us mad if we fall into the trap of prioritising them over what comes up on the way. This is what John Krakauer, in his story of the 1996 Everest disaster, *Into Thin Air*, painfully calls out. Climbers in a desperate desire to reach the top failed to see changing conditions and in 24 hours eight people died. We have to get beyond being fixated on a pre-set goal. A plant grows up towards the moving sun and finds its way. Instead of fixing on a destination, all we need is a sense of direction.

Goal focus is also limiting. As someone with an active imagination, I tend to see possibilities that are far beyond me. Quite apart from the constant disappointment caused when they do not materialise, in focusing on them I tend to miss the more obvious things right in front of me. Instead I'd characterise this committed but open-to-change movement as a 'coodiwomple' – a beautiful English slang word that means to travel purposefully toward an as yet unknown place. This is the broad space in the sky that we sketch as our direction of travel, rather than becoming fixed on any one particular destination. If things come up on the way, we can then be open to them.

In this we have to accept that, as an explorer, part of the badge of office is that we may feel lost, uncertain and fearful for a while. This not knowing, as well as being a hardship, is also the reward. In our loosely held quest, it is part of the job requirement to be able to cope with the less well-lit moments. In order to find something new we have to pad about in the dark a bit. This liminal space between dusk and dawn is natural and has to be expected, because we are not following someone else. We are having to find our own route rather than following one that already exists. The trick is to see that clarity usually comes soon after the point at which we feel the confusion most heavily. Knowing this, we can embrace complexity more readily. Suddenly, as we turn a corner on the path, the fog clears and a breakthrough occurs. When we find something truly amazing, we see that we got here because we emptied ourselves of what we previously knew first.

In this frame of mind, we will find ourselves stepping into green and verdant fields busy with growth, where the path is not obvious. That is because there is no path. We are creating our own path through the field with each step that we make. This is what creating anew is like. At any time, we can take a step back onto a more established track, and from there we can find a roadway and eventually a motorway. But any change is about leaving the familiar, well-signed trunk road of habits that we usually travel on. At first it is hard because the mind sees obstacles in every challenge and creates fear out of every opportunity. By learning to accept and see more we start to appreciate the richness of possibility that lies in every small step. The danger is that we look ahead too far, searching for assurance. This encourages our mind to worry that there is no path instead of allowing us to settle in the joy of making one. It is not by the mind's doing but by the work of making one step after another that we create our path.

As we forge our way through the fresh field of growth, what we can do is to watch our mind rather than be controlled by it. We can see it for what it is, a useful member of the team, not the one in charge. When it screams at us with good intent, in an effort to defend us, we can listen to it and calm it. We can see the stories it creates for what they are: a defensive narrative that would have us go back to safety. 'I hear what you are saying,' we can say, 'and thank you for that – here is what I am going to do', as we work out how to take the next step, slowly making our way through the high grass. As we do, we see the colours of the wild grasses and the butterflies fluttering about us. We take a long breath and smell the fresh air. Once we have done this for a while and have got used to it, we look back to the motorway. We might even slip back onto it briefly in a lapse. But we don't chide ourselves for this; instead we learn from it and grow strength for the decision we have now committed to. We see that the old tracks and the motorway were not good for us. In time, we realise that the motorway is itself growing over. It is only now, as we travel more and more easily, that we see the new route we have created as the clear path that it now is.

In this framework, what might have once become our fear doesn't disappear or get conquered. It transforms. It becomes our guide and our challenge in a supportive environment, where we feel able to engage with what might have been a monster as a friend. Because we have changed and are now calmly walking towards it, we see that this monster wasn't real anyway. It was something we created in our original fear.

A truly enabled approach gives us far more than just a means to reframe our fears. Through this lens we get a different conceptual, linguistic and behavioural approach rooted in the very nature from where we originally came. It isn't that we ever left the Garden of Eden, it is still here. In our own *viriditas*, if somewhat buried at times, it lives on.

Ultimately, Enabled Power gives us the possibility of a great reconnection and a new sense of original belonging in place of the narrative of original sin. This is what John Stewart Collis meant when he talked about realising the unity of life on a different level of understanding. That unity is there already. We just have to embrace it.

What is your taproot?

# 10. Next Steps

It was a busy morning at King's Cross station. The more recently built northern entrance to the underground station was rammed full as maybe two or three hundred people slowly filed in lines through the barriers at the top of the hall. In a mixture of jostling for position and politeness up close, we all had a clear destination in mind. Once we were through, the crowds accelerated towards the banks of escalators and down into the vast underground cavern. We were all full of intent, moving towards our various morning goals.

I walked down, taking the furthest left of the three or four escalators and, as I did so, I heard music. I felt some familiarity with the piece but it was a complicated arrangement and not what I'd normally expect, whatever that was. As I came to the bottom of the escalator I saw why; with a round, many-stringed guitar, an interesting player stood off to my far right, playing alone.

When I reached the bottom, I followed the mass of people off to the Victoria and Piccadilly lines. As I walked down the tunnel, following with everyone else, it slowly dawned what the tune was. It was the theme tune to 'The Snowman', performed on this fine day in May. It was done so beautifully I hardly recognised it save for the odd choruses poking through.

It was one thing to choose to be in this cavern at this time on a bright May morning with these columns of fast-moving people in some Orwellian vision, but it was another thing to give myself up to that flow entirely. Much as I had a destination and an appointment, I could increasingly feel that something was pulling at me. I knew I wasn't happy to just follow the track I was on.

Then, in an instant, I got clarity on something that had not previously been clear. I would regret it somewhere in the deep-down soul of who I was if I didn't make an effort to acknowledge this man, the player. Having a thought wasn't enough without an action. Nobody would know what I thought, especially the player. In order to have any impact, I needed to act. The instinct to act had always been there, but something in me had managed to supress it.

By this point I was far down the long cavern, nearing a minute or so of walking away from the open space where the musician played. I had moved on. I was deep in a crowd of people heading for the stairs to the Tube platform. As these various thoughts started to affect me, I made an on-the-spot decision – I decided to go back.

As I completed the 180-degree turn and joined the flow of people who had been on my right, moving in the opposite direction, I noticed that how I felt about what I was doing had changed. I knew now that doing this one small thing was far more important than keeping to my self-imposed schedule, to be in good time for my appointment.

As I walked back I felt in my pockets for coins. I had none. Maybe I had a five-pound note, I thought. A quick inspection of my bills revealed only twenties. No realistic money, I realised. Isn't that why I am going back? Part of me was momentarily confused. There was no question that I was going back – but why was I doing so, if not to give the busker some money, as he surely wanted?

As I came back into the wide space at the bottom of the escalator where the player was, 'The Snowman' gently came to an end. The underground cavern opened up again and I stopped feeling any residual uncertainty about my actions. Instead, I felt a perfect fit between who I was and what I was doing which had not been there before. If I had done what I had subsequently viewed to be the right thing in the first place, I would not have arrived at the musician at any point close to his natural pause. Through my more laboured indirect route I was arriving, here and now, for a good reason. The cogs of action and reaction in the world were somehow aligned.

In the pause, I walked straight up to the man and said, 'I am sorry, I don't have any coins on me but just wanted to say that I really enjoyed your playing. It was beautiful and it gave a lift to my morning.' The man, who looked Spanish or South American, had a deep twinkle in his eyes as he looked at me and said, 'My friend, thank you.' There was a glow of warmth in his rugged face as he reached out to me with his hand and said, 'Can I shake your hand?'

As we shook hands I felt something emotional connect between us. His eyes glistened and through his hand I felt a tingle of joy. As I walked away, back up the tunnel towards my train, I could feel a sense of excitement flow through my entire body. Part of it was that I had followed what I knew to be an authentic path for me. But the much bigger piece was that I was part of something that morning for him. Together, we were something much greater than we ever could be apart.

Fear Hack works like this walk. It starts because we pick up on a clue. We build an appreciation for something important for us. We might suppress it initially, but we then enter a dialogue between the comfort of staying as we are, in the track we are in, and turning to explore the thing that calls to us. As we contemplate the turn we might see the track we are in now and the structure that we feel either imposes on us or we choose to impose on ourselves. We might notice the texture of the comfort we feel now and why it has a hold on us. We can also notice any uncertainty or discomfort we feel as we turn towards the thing that attracts or challenges us. In our safe state, we see any such discomfort as a good sign.

The next steps, for each of us, also work like this. Unfortunately, lovely though it would be, there is no set of easy answers telling us what to do. Our anchor is our connection with the world outside of us and the clues there that are calling for our active engagement. Our next steps come from our own sensing of what that call means. Risk, change, loss, difficulty and pain can all feature in what we find. It is by embracing these and our deepest fears that our greatest growth, and ultimately our joy, lies.

As soon as we commit to the turn and start to walk towards what we fear, the process of learning from it starts. As we progress towards and then through it, we will usually find that the experience is different from what our mind told us. As the ultimate captain of our ship, having just taken a decision, noticing this helps us to assess the value of the counsel our wider crew gives us. We see it as an input to respect, not as something we have to immediately respond to out of knee-jerk habit.

As we ride in the saddle of the challenge we also make sure that we keep our eyes open and enjoy the ride. This is not about getting to a destination, it is being open to what we find and learning from the experience. The work is its own reward and, once we are here, we also find that we are more resilient to its challenges than our mind allowed us to realise when we first contemplated this move. We also find that the moment is always different to what we anticipate. As we trust our ability to cope in that moment as it evolves, we tend to realise that we can act and think on our feet more than our mind would have us believe.

The tingle of joy I had as I finally walked away from the player came out of a connection, made in that instant, which meant something to us both. In this subterranean cavern of a place, surrounded by busy commuter traffic, we'd managed, between us, to carry and create a safe space. For me, I had fulfilled my instinct to convey to the player what I felt he was adding to the world instead of letting it bottle up inside me, where it meant nothing to him. For him, I felt he got something significant out of knowing that he was being heard and appreciated. The sense I had was that he had grown a little bit stronger and taller as he beamed back at me. He'd left me in no doubt that I should do it again. I also knew this because I felt a buzz of excitement rising within me. The energy released in that moment went on to ricochet through my day. It showed up in the strategy work I went on to do that afternoon for a client and still shows up in the core of who I am, in some small part, to this day.

Changing the lens of power through which we see has a critical effect. Everything we do shows up differently. We look for and see signs of growth everywhere. Instead of looking for weakness in others, we see their strengths. We enable others to grow not by hectoring them from our perspective but by holding them to their own possibility in theirs. When we communicate through the lens of Enabled Power we listen rather more than we talk. When we come to negotiate, we ask rather than tell. When we lead, we cede responsibility rather than holding on to power and giving directions on every matter. We instead pride ourselves on creating a vision that everyone understands and knows how to apply to their role. Everything we do, we do to allow others to grow. In turn, others do the same for us. In this reframing of our narrative structure, it is not just fear that changes. Once we realise the power we have and embrace our fears as the stuff of growth, we all get to face confidently outward, together. In this form, fear is part of the gift of consciousness. It shows us that the most fearful of us might simply have this gift in profusion, in the form of highly fertile and creative imaginations. The question is how we see this gift and how we choose to use it – for it is a choice.

A few weeks after the fire at Grenfell Tower in London in June 2017, I attended an event in North London that had been convened to discuss how communities might go about building their own initiatives from the grassroots. As the afternoon developed the event broke into what is called an 'open space' session, where anyone has the opportunity to propose a topic and to encourage people to join a group to discuss that topic. At first the flow of suggestions was slow but it soon sped up as people saw the possibility that the session presented. There were a lot of unhappy people in the room and their anger found a vent.

As the suggestions came in there were some great ideas. In the confusion, I started to listen not just to the words but to what the people talking made me feel. I had no idea which I would pick until a young woman, who had clearly also been listening and taking it all in, stood up and said that she wanted to propose a group to talk about doing something rather than talking about anything. I liked the idea and, more importantly, I liked the way she conveyed the idea. Rather than being angry, she radiated commitment, and I was keen to find out what ideas she had.

Once in the group I found myself surrounded by women who were mostly, at my guess, of African or Caribbean origin. The woman proposing the group turned out to be from the Grenfell Tower community and she explained what she and her neighbours were doing in the direct aftermath of the disaster. The talking inevitably took over and although we shared some ideas about how we might create something new rather than simply fighting the status quo, this was not the place for doing anything.

It was therefore a relief when another woman, Mama D, proposed that we find a way to express how we felt through movement rather than in any more words. Although most accepted the idea, some wanted to refine it, so the discussion in a way continued. Finally, a few of us got up and accepted the suggestion wholeheartedly by moving. Soon seven of us were standing, waiting for instructions.

The exercise turned out to be largely in our imaginations, as Mama D asked us to close our eyes and to take ourselves back to the first dawn on a barren planet, stripped back of anything we knew. Once we found ourselves fully in that space, we were encouraged to feel the first stirrings of the morning as the sun made the promise of impending light to us. As the sun slowly rose we were encouraged to feel the effect of the light and to enjoy and move into the possibility of the new world that was dawning before us and of which we were a part.

I sank into the exercise and found it remarkably easy to connect with something deep inside me that without any thought at all gave me movement and shape as I formed an obvious and natural way of engaging with the world around me. As the exercise started to come to a natural end I became curious, with my eyes still shut, to find out where all the others were and what it meant for them.

As we opened our eyes together, all of us went through a surprised and startled moment when we realised that we were all making the basically the same shape. All of us had our hands up, outstretched, with our fingers spread in the shape of a tree. Our bodies were open, stretching out for possibility, for light and for connection. The only difference I noticed was that two of the group were no longer standing but were on bended knees, almost reaching out for each other.

The sense of togetherness we'd all felt quickly started to dissipate, as it wasn't long before people's hands started to fall, mine among them. With our eyes shut and our deepest instincts encouraged to come alive we had experienced something in this safe space that held an insight. That glimpse lived on, but I did notice how quickly the shapes we had made moments before had easily fallen down under the fluorescent lights of the old hall.

I later learned that Mama D works with a community organisation called 'Ubele', which is derived from the Swahili for 'the future'. Ubele is a community-building organisation that seeks to increase the capacity of the African diaspora community in the UK to lead and to create their own social initiatives from the ground up. Tired of waiting for the central or local government to help people, they are help-ing people to help themselves.

The exercise helped me feel and understand how I continually need to move myself back into the open, reaching-out shape and person that I was that afternoon. I lost it so easily as my eyes reopened to the structure of the day, just as it is easy to lose it in the everyday chal-lenges of a modern busy life.

Perhaps the feeling we have historically chosen to call fear will never be entirely gone, but with Enabled Power, its narrative can be completely rewritten. The rewards are there, and it is in the facing of our own particular challenges, and the difficulties that we experience in taking them on, that growth is to be found.

The good news is that finding it again has just become a great deal easier.

What exciting thing is next for you?

# Acknowledgements

There are many people to be thanked for the ideas and experiences that make up this book, including all those who have ever attended a Friday Club or a Fear Hack. My research method is mainly to listen to what is happening. This means the rather diverse source material comes from just about anywhere. You know who you are and thank you all. In particular I'd like to thank the brilliantly creative purplesime, aka Simon White, whose original idea finally set me off and who provided a sounding board throughout.

Thank you also to my inspiring early partners in the workshop, Alison Sayers and Kay Scorah, both of whom stretched me creatively in ways I needed to be and without whom I wouldn't have got anywhere like so far. Special thanks must go to the ever insightful and thankfully rather brave Nick Parker who finally helped me to bring what I thought were two separate things together and to see what this book really was. Dan Kieran gave me much needed thoughtful insight on the early drafts as did Miranda West and my brother, Marcus Gallo.

Thank you to the team at Unbound for all your help, including Xander Cansell in particular. This book would not be half as good as it is without the help of editor Miranda Ward, whose observations helped me to move everything up a gear or two, and Andrew Chapman, who helped me find overdrive. Finally, I'd like to thank my wife Ina together with Lucas and Anna for their contributions (and putting up with the whole process) and finally, finally to everyone who backed the book at Unbound and allowed it to become real. This only leaves the unnamed person I also want to thank – the original kid with the dinosaur who gave a new perspective to the whole frightful thing. Thank you.

# Patrons

M AlQurashi
Carolina Arriagada
Stuart Ashen
Matt Ballantine
Elizabeth Barrett
Alex Bell
Adrian Briggs
Anke Buchta
Rodica Bugaian
Dan Bull
Matt Butcher
Tim Butler
Steve Chapman
Sue Coulthard
David Culling
Katie Elliott
Charles Fernyhough
Aldo Framingo
Jamie Fraser
Mark Goodier
Max Gooding
Kate Gregory
Eamonn Griffin
Nick Hammond
Jayne Harrison
Andrew Hearse
Sara Houston
Jo Howard
Hilary Jeanes
Arpit Kaushik
Christina Kennedy
Andrew Leahy

Mark Lloyd
Stephen Lockyer
Gemma Lodge
Jonny Miller
Nick Mitchell
Kim Monney
Alison Navarro
Carlo Navato
Al Nicholson
David Nolan
Leonora Oppenheim
Nick Osborne
Paul Osgood
Annelise Pesa
Steve Peters
Sam Phillips
Ioana Popescu
Stefan Powell
Robert Poynton
Antony Quinn
Emma Sajben
Kay Scorah
Stephanie Scott
Laurence Shapiro
Thomas Sherlaw
Stanley Skoglund
Claerwen Snell
Dave Sox
Catherine Stavrakis
Sara Taheri
Bea Tartsanyi
Neil Taylor
Olga Vysotska
Marc Weymann
John V Willshire

James Wilson
Doug Wood

The cover of this book was designed using output produced in a workshop held at Accept & Proceed in Hackney, London on July 25th, 2018. The participants were Freya Smith, Nigel Cottier, Brittany Miller, David Johnston, Anna Gallo and Hilary Gallo.

Hilary had previously done a Fear Hack workshop with the team at Accept & Proceed and we were all keen to experience how fear impacts the creative process. This included us experiencing actual physical fear together with fear of failure and fear of losing control. What we feared was that we might lock ourselves into the certainty of what we knew and we wanted to find ways to open this up. In particular, we decided to do a loose series of activities where any sense of ownership for the task in hand or the overall outcome was distributed randomly. Ultimately, we were hoping to transcend the ego through these processes. We wanted to be free to create freely without any of our individual monkey minds on the one hand or any established collective path, on the other, taking over.

**Activity 1** Straightaway, we left the studio for the local park, Hackney Downs, and a climbing frame. Who wanted to go first? The invitation was to hang upside down whilst performing a series of tasks. We all felt the fear as we hung there, with our heads a few feet off the ground. First, we were given a rather lethal sharp knife and invited to cut away at the word FEAR on a pad of paper. Then we were invited to draw a perfect circle. We all noticed that having a purpose helped us. Our fear disappeared whilst we were focused on the task. The moment the job was complete and our minds were free again, the fear came rushing back and we wanted to get down.

**Activity 2** This task saw us playing with control and ownership. We were given a series of shapes and asked to compose them on a page with no specific rationale. As a next step our work was passed along for someone else to build upon. Slowly through the process of the workshop we realised that we were creating typography. A whole alphabet was created by the end of it but with no participant knowing that was where we were going with it. The usual aesthetic

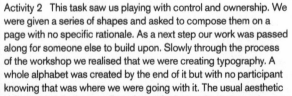

judgement calls that we all tend to make in the creative process were removed completely. Our designs emerged without any selective or judgemental limits. It felt like a true collaboration.

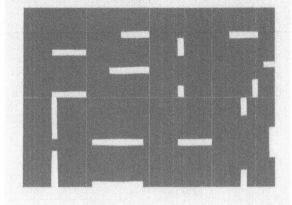

Activity 3   Using some pre-prepared materials and anything else that lay to hand, we were asked to hack, deconstruct, or assemble forms that spoke into a hand manipulated hacking design process. We cut, curled, folded and even drowned fear in the kitchen sink. In the age of computer generated design the results were immediately different. They felt refreshing, honest, raw and human. It gave us confidence to see what we were truly capable of when we turned the technology dial down and the human volume up.

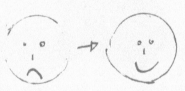

Activity 4   This activity saw us creating designs at a crazy speed. How could we capture the essence of what this was about really quickly? Then it got faster. With so little time, the time to doubt left us along with any time to think. We had 5 seconds, then 3 seconds and finally all of 1 second to generate a design. Cutting everything down to its essence yielded more insightful results than our thought heavy minds would ever have allowed us to expect.